A GENIUS

FOR WAR

EMORY UPTON IN THE CIVIL WAR

BY

PETER S. MICHIE

PROFESSOR U.S. MILITARY ACADEMY

WITH AN INTRODUCTION

BY

JAMES HARRISON WILSON

1885

Contents

PREFACE

The subject of the following memoir was widely known by reputation in the military profession, and the story of his life would, at least to military men, have been a matter of passing interest. The tragic circumstances of his death seemed to demand some explanation in harmony with his established reputation and character. At the earnest solicitation of his nearest relatives, the author, although conscious of his own deficiencies, undertook the task of compiling a brief record of General Upton's life for his family and immediate personal friends.

In overstepping the limits at first proposed for the work, and in extending its circulation to the general public, the author has been guided by two considerations: First, the hope that the lessons drawn from General Upton's life might be valuable to the youths who may hereafter enter the military profession, brought about a modification of its original plan, and necessitated the omission of much that was of purely family interest; second, Upton's valuable researches into the military policy of his country, and the essential influence which his conclusions will have upon its future military organizations, seemed to warrant the wider publicity which is now attempted.

Although the volume has been written while the author has been engaged in official duties of a somewhat exacting nature, his task has been greatly lessened by the abundant material placed at his disposal. Whatever excellence the book contains, the author gratefully acknowledges to be due to the wise counsel and able criticism of his friend General J. H. Wilson. Whatever defects honest criticism may note in the matter retained, method of presentation, or style of expression, are to be charged to the inexperience of the author, whose only qualification for the assumed task was a sincere desire to judge rightly and deal justly with the character of his friend and comrade.

INTRODUCTION

It was my good fortune to know Emory Upton from the date of his entry into the Military Academy at West Point, as a mere stripling, in 1856, to the time of his death, in the full maturity of his manhood, in 1881.

Upton, a longtime sufferer of severe headaches, took his own life on March 15, 1881.—Ed. 2016

His class was next to mine, graduated less than a year afterward, and entered the army at the outbreak of the great rebellion. We served together during the Antietam campaign; then in Grant's memorable series of operations from the Rapidan to Petersburg; then with Sheridan in the Valley of Virginia; and, finally, in the cavalry campaign from Waterloo through Alabama and Georgia, ending in the last battles of the war and the collapse of the Confederacy. From the close associations of these nine years of youth and early manhood, and especially of the last year of the rebellion, during which Upton commanded a division of cavalry under my immediate supervision, I came to know him with that intimacy which is possible only between soldiers. After the war our paths lay apart, for, while I resumed my duties as an engineer officer, and finally left the army altogether for the purpose of building and operating railroads, Upton, although urged to resign and engage in private business, on the theory that it was as meritorious for a man of his parts to leave the army in times of peace as to enter it in times of war, after mature consideration declined, and determined to devote himself for life to the military profession. He realized that, while his campaigning days were probably over, there was yet a brilliant career open for him in the writing of tactics, the study of the organization and administration of armies, and in the evolution of an effective and economical military policy for our Government. As shown by the course of the narrative which follows, he served after the close of the war successively on the Plains; as commandant of cadets at West Point; on a board of officers to assimilate the tactics of artillery, cavalry, and infantry; as the head of a commission to visit Asia and Europe for the purpose of inspecting and reporting upon the armies of those countries; as superintendent of theoretical instruction in the Artillery School for Practice at Fortress Monroe; and, finally, in command of his regiment in California. During the whole of this time we corresponded with each other, and our friendly relations remained unbroken to the end.

The history of the events which occurred during the War of the Rebellion is fast being written, and is of great importance to the American people, but it needs the element of personality to give it that absorbing interest which is necessary to fix it in the mind, and to impress its lessons upon the understanding of coming generations. Fortunately for the country, the pages of history can never be illuminated by a more exemplary character or a more spotless name than that of Upton. His life was pure and unselfish in the highest degree, and yet it was controlled by a patriotic and sleepless ambition, accompanied by an ardent love for the profession of arms, which, from their earliest dawn, filled him with the resolve to acquire military fame. This idea dominated him completely throughout his career, and when the rebellion broke out it found the young soldier not only ready, but eager for the fray. His loyalty to the Constitution and the Union was unshakable; it was bone of his bone and blood of his blood. His courage and independence had already been proved by sturdy resistance to the arrogance of his Southern classmates. He had at his very advent at the Academy boldly announced that he was an abolitionist, and in sympathy with whatever tended to promote the freedom of the slaves. He had been ostracized for his political opinions, and had suffered in body and mind for his superiority to sectional influences. He had been forced to fight because he would not bend before the blustering bravado of the "fire-eaters," and had come off victorious. He had grown in strength of intellect as well as of body; he had made his way from the foot of his class, where the alphabetical arrangement had placed him, to the first section, where he graduated. He entered the army with a strong, healthy, robust constitution, full of energy and courage, and with a well-trained mind richly stored with such knowledge as he could obtain from text-books, and, what was more and quite unusual, he had the faculty of turning this knowledge promptly' and efficiently to practical use in his profession.

This was one of his strongest points. He was proud and honorable, and feared no man; his love of God was open and avowed; his love of liberty for all God's creatures amounted to a passion, and, while his love for his chosen profession was deep-seated and abiding, it found its justification to himself in the opportunity it would give him, during the trials which had come upon the nation, to render good service to the cause of humanity and to that of his country's unity. But aside from patriotism on the one hand and religion on the other, he was a genuine military enthusiast, whose thoughts night and day turned to the art of war. No knight of old was ever more absorbed in dreams of military glory, nor more grimly determined to win it, as opportunity offered. He was tremendously in earnest, and whatever his hand found to do, that he did with all his might. Had Upton lived during the period of any of the great European wars, he might still have been a devout, God-fearing Christian, but he would certainly have been a soldier, and with favoring circumstances he would have been a great captain. His ambition, subordinated and controlled as it was by a character of extraordinary purity and strength, was limited only by his sense of duty as a soldier and as a patriot. Like the young eagle which had not yet felt the strength of its pinions, there was no flight within the range of his vision which he would hesitate to essay. At the very outset of his career this was plain to those who knew him well, and, long before the war of the rebellion ended, it had come to be understood by all that there was no enterprise too perilous for Upton, if only he might hope to gain credit or promotion thereby. No proper understanding can be had of Upton's character without giving full force and effect to this peculiarity. He had as high a sense of duty as any man, and would have cheerfully laid down his life and all its anticipations of honor and fame in the performance of any service for his country which its legally constituted authorities could have set for him, but throughout his career he was constantly inspired and cheered by the thought of "young ambition's ladder," whereto he upward turned his face in order that he might reach its topmost round. It must be said, however, that as he rose from round to round he neither turned his

4

back upon the ladder, nor scorned the degrees by which he did ascend. He was modest at all times, constant, courageous, and vigilant. He was loyal and obedient to his superiors whoever they were, though his patience was more than once severely tested by what seemed to him indifference or incompetence on the part of those above him. He did all in his power to improve the discipline and to promote the subordination of the army to those in authority over it. He had no disposition to take part in cliques or cabals, but felt that it was his duty to serve in silence wherever he might be sent, and to be faithful over those things which might be confided to his care.

With an ample education given him by his country, inspired by the enthusiasm of youth, and guided by the correct principles of manhood, Upton began his public career fully equipped, and under the most favorable auspices. He was not long in realizing his ambitious dreams, for honorable mention and rapid promotion followed close upon his intrepid deeds. As a regimental drill-master, and as an aide-de-camp, battery commander, and chief of artillery, he shared all the perils of the Army of the Potomac in the earlier days of the war, gaining experience and familiarity with military operations in the field, and above all gaining confidence in himself and his own military knowledge and capacity, as compared with those of the officers with whom he was thrown in contact. His voluminous correspondence with his family and friends gives abundant evidence of the readiness with which he advanced from details to the higher considerations of administration and command, and even to those of strategy and military policy. He soon saw that, having devoted five years to acquiring the education of a soldier, and having participated in the first battle of Bull Run, and the subsequent operations in Virginia, he knew just as much about war as an art and science as the older officers of the regular army, and a great deal more than was possible for any officer of volunteers fresh and green from civil life. This encouraged him to believe that notwithstanding his youth—for at the outbreak of hostilities he was only twenty-two years old—and in spite of his lack of political influence, he would surely gain rank if his life were spared. This last consideration was of the first importance to him, as to all ambitious soldiers, for the chances of death were very great in the war then raging. Upton had early become convinced that the first requisite to success in the profession of arms was unflinching and unhesitating courage, not only for its influence over his superiors, but over those whom he had to lead, and yet observation taught him that the most courageous were frequently the first to fall. Fully appreciating all the dangers of his calling, he never shirked one of them, but boldly and resolutely met them wherever and whenever duty seemed to require it of him. He was neither rash nor foolhardy, and yet the closest observer could find nothing in his conduct under fire to criticise. His courage was both physical and moral, and therefore of the highest type. When he reported to me for assignment to the command of a division of cavalry, he remarked that he had no doubt of his professional capacity to manage cavalry as well as either artillery or infantry, but he expressed considerable anxiety as to his standing with his division until he should have commanded it in action and shown both officers and men that he was neither afraid nor lacking in dash. He feared that the rigid discipline he would exact and the constant instruction he would give might for a while make him unpopular, but he felt sure that he would remove all prejudice of that sort at the first action in which he should lead his division. The result was as he anticipated in every respect, except as to his unpopularity. The division to which he was assigned was composed of veterans, who saw from the start that his was a master-hand. Both men and officers responded promptly and cheerfully to every demand he made upon them, and after the fights at Montevallo and Plantersville, the assault upon Selma, and the capture of Columbus, by a night attack of extraordinary brilliancy, their confidence in and admiration for him were unbounded. They felt that under his leadership they could go anywhere and do anything, while he told me that he had learned the greatest lesson of his life, in reference to the relative value of the three arms of service, and as to the almost boundless capacity of mounted troops when properly armed, organized, and commanded. Immediately after the capture of Columbus, to which I shall allude again, he declared that he could traverse the Confederacy from end to end, and from side to side, with his single division, carrying any kind of fortifications by assault with which he might come in contact, and defying capture by any kind or amount of force which might be sent against him. This declaration was not that of a braggart, but was the honest conclusion at which he had arrived, after the closest observation and reflection. In the hour of battle he was as intrepid a man as ever drew a saber, and yet in battle, as well as on the march or in camp, prudence and judgment were his constant companions. He left nothing to chance, and trusted nothing to mere luck, but provided for everything, and as far as possible foresaw everything. He knew that discipline, order, and attention to the details of organization, equipment, and supply, whether on the march of in the camp, were essential to success in a long-continued campaign, and would do more than everything else toward making his command invincible in action. He did not for a moment commit the fault, so common to young cavalry-commanders, of supposing that he could build up a solid reputation by courage and enterprise alone. He saw that both men and horses required constant attention; that celerity of movement, compactness of formation, and long-continued exertion, were no less essential than courage in action, and that no amount of the latter could compensate for lack of condition on the part of either men or horses, or their equipment. Hence, from the day he took command of his division its improvement in every respect was conspicuous, and, what is more important, this improvement continued to show itself throughout the campaign, which ended at Augusta, Georgia. At that time the condition of his division was all that could be desired, and it may be doubted if it was in any respect surpassed by that of any other cavalry division in the army, although it had been under his command less than three months.

But to return to the earlier days of Upton's career. His experience in the command of a battery of horse-artillery, at the siege of Yorktown, the action at West Point, and at the battles of Gaines's Mills and Glendale, and also in command of a brigade of artillery in the Maryland campaign, was of the most creditable character. It brought him prominently into notice; but; owing to the broken and heavily wooded condition of most of the Virginia battlefields, and the consequent limitations upon the use of artillery, he saw that that arm would not afford him scope enough for his genius, and that, the

7

more useful he made himself in it, the less chance would he have for service in the other arms, or for promotion to the rank of a general officer. Consequently he spared no proper effort to secure the command of a regiment of infantry, and did not rest till he had got it. This gave him a larger field for usefulness, together with an abundance of that kind of work which he coveted and for which he was peculiarly fitted. His first care was to secure the confidence of his regiment, and this he did by showing it that he knew his business in all its details, whether in camp, on the march, or in battle. His constant effort was to keep it well supplied, properly clad, and under perfect drill and discipline, and so successful was he in all this that he soon became noted throughout the Army of the Potomac as a model colonel. He was one of the few officers in service who properly appreciated the value of an address to his men before going into battle, and it was his custom to encourage them in this way whenever occasion offered.

It is not my purpose to follow him through the details of his service as regimental commander, extending from October 23, 1862, to July 4, 1863. This has been done in the narrative which follows. The command of a brigade came to him in due time, not only by seniority as a colonel, but by the selection of those in authority over him, and his conduct in the still broader field which it opened was characterized by the same fertility of resource, untiring zeal, and attention to details that had hitherto distinguished him. No duty was omitted. Drill, discipline, and order were exacted from all, and supervised by him in all the regiments under his command. Tactics and formations for battle were most carefully studied, and nothing was left to chance. Every order was executed by him with the greatest possible precision, and when left to himself he provided for every contingency, including that of success as well as that of failure. As a consequence, it soon came to be understood that Upton's brigade must lead all attacks and assaults made within his reach, and, what was of still greater credit to him, he rarely failed to carry the enemy's position, whether fortified or not. This was not mere chance, nor was it altogether the result of intrepidity and dash. He showed those qualities in the highest degree, but he showed prudent foresight and good judgment, combined with careful preparation for every step of the undertaking assigned to him, in a still higher degree. In view of the splendid fighting qualities of the rebel Army of Northern Virginia, and of the great vigilance and abilities displayed by Lee and his subordinate commanders of every grade, and considering the extraordinary mortality that always attended an engagement with them, it may well be doubted if the metal of any soldier of modern times was ever more severely tested than was Upton's during his two years' service in the Army of the Potomac, and especially at Salem Heights, Rappahannock Station, in the Wilderness, or while leading the assaulting column of twelve regiments of the Sixth Corps which carried the Angle of the enemy's intrenchments at Spottsylvania. The abilities displayed by him on this occasion were of the highest character, and secured for him not only the praises of the whole army, but the long-coveted and amply earned reward of a commission as brigadier-general of volunteers, and also as brevet lieutenant-colonel in the regular army. But neither the hard work nor the hard knocks were over yet. He displayed the same high qualities in all the movements, marches, and battles which characterized that remarkable campaign, including the bloody actions of Cold Harbor and the siege and assaults of the rebel works about Petersburg. His conduct throughout these trying times was absolutely faultless; while his cheerful and unshaken confidence in the ultimate success of our arms had a great influence on those about him, and was worthy of all praise. He was prompt and obedient at all times and in all situations, and his alacrity was surpassed only by the resolution and the steadiness which he displayed in the desperate and almost constant fighting in which the army was engaged for nearly a year after Grant took command. He gave loyal and unquestioning support to his superior officers, and especially to those who were in chief command; but it must not be supposed that he was a mere machine soldier, or that he gave his approval to their plans as he gave obedience to their orders. He studiously and carefully refrained from public criticism, but he was too good an officer and too close a student of the art of war to blindly shut his eyes to the faults which were committed about him. The fact is, that he saw much to condemn in the daily operations of the army, and the reader will not fail to note that his active mind poured itself out in criticism in his letters to his sister. It was to her that he expressed his disappointment at the long delay of his promotion to the rank of brigadier-general after he had earned it over and over again; it was to her that he wrote during the overland campaign: "Our men have in many instances been foolishly and wantonly sacrificed. Assault after assault has been ordered upon the enemy's intrenchments when [the general ordering it] knew nothing about the strength or position of the enemy. Thousands of lives might have been spared by the exercise of a little skill; but as it is, the courage of the poor men is expected to obviate all difficulties. I must confess that, so long as I see such incompetency, there is no grade in the army to which I do not aspire." It was also to her he wrote: "We are now at Cold Harbor, where we have been since June 1st. On that day we had a murderous engagement. I say murderous, because we were recklessly ordered to assault the enemy's intrenchments"; and again: "I am very sorry to say I have seen but little generalship during the campaign. Some of our corps commanders are not fit to be corporals. Lazy and incompetent, they will not even ride along their lines; yet without hesitancy they will order us to attack the enemy, no matter what their position or what their numbers. Twenty thousand of our killed and wounded should today be in our ranks." But it will not escape the reader's attention that Upton's mind was not content at this period to confine itself to the mere condemnation of details. It was incessantly occupied in trying to work out correct solutions for all the military problems then engaging the army's attention; and while subsequent events did not justify all his suggestions or criticisms, the careful student of the war will be struck by the extraordinary grasp and ability displayed in the arguments and conclusions which he so patiently recounted, perhaps for his own improvement as much as for the information and instruction of his sister. Nor will the reader fail to note that as early as June 5, 1864, when Upton was not yet twenty-five years of age, he had not only detected and pointed out the crude methods and incompetency which were so prevalent, but had frankly, and with pardonable ambition, declared that there was no grade in the army to which he did not aspire.

When Lee detached Early to threaten Washington and harry the Maryland border, it was Upton's good fortune to be sent in the same direction with the Sixth Corps, to which his brigade was attached. He took part in all the operations for the relief and defense of the capital, and finally participated in the battle of the Opequan and the capture of Winchester, in which Early's army was completely routed. It was Upton's brigade which first deployed on the plateau beyond the Opequan after its capture by the cavalry. It was his brigade and the cavalry division which covered the debouchment of the Sixth Corps from the defile through which it was compelled to advance, and held the field till it and the rest of the army could deploy and form for the attack. It was his brigade which, by a change of front to the right, arrested the flight of a part of the Sixth and Nineteenth Corps, and, taking the enemy in flank, drove them back in confusion. It was also his brigade which, in the final rush of both infantry and cavalry, pierced the enemy's left center, and made the victory both certain and complete. It was in this charge that the heroic General David A. Russell, commanding the division, was mortally wounded. He was promptly succeeded by Upton, who pressed the division forward with conspicuous ability and energy. In the full tide of success the gallant young commander was severely wounded on the inside of the right thigh by a fragment of a bursting shell. The muscle was frightfully lacerated and the femoral artery laid bare, but, instead of retiring, as he was fully justified in doing, and indeed as he was ordered to do by General Sheridan in person, he called his staff-surgeon and directed him to stanch the bleeding wound by a tourniquet. As soon as this was done, he called for a stretcher, and had himself borne about the field thereon, still directing the movements of his victorious division, and did not leave it or give up the command till night had put an end to the pursuit. The fortitude displayed by him upon this occasion was heroic in the extreme, and marked him as a man of extraordinary nerve. It was in notable contrast with what had come to be customary on such occasions. So bloody had been the Richmond campaign under Grant, that both officers and men counted themselves fortunate when they received a slight wound, which might be honorably availed of as an excuse for leaving the field, and thus escaping the

11

peril of a mortal one. I knew a corps commander of the Army of the Potomac, in the earlier days of the war, famed for his fighting qualities, who retired from battle because of a trifling flesh-wound under the arch of the right foot, and who peremptorily refused to return to the line, although he was urged to do so, if need be, in an ambulance or on a stretcher, in order that his corps might be rallied around him, and possibly avert a great disaster, if it did not win a great victory'. Few men have had such an opportunity for fame. Had it fallen to Upton's lot, can anyone doubt that he would have availed himself of it, even if his foot had been taken off, instead of being so slightly wounded that he could have walked upon it, as did the corps commander in less than six days? Fortitude on the part of a general upon such occasions is the greatest of military virtues. It inflames the soldiers with enthusiasm, and inspires them with courage as nothing else can.

This battle, which had won for Upton the command of a division, closed his career as a leader of infantry in the Union army. His wound was so severe that he was entirely disabled by it till the middle of December following. Meanwhile I had been assigned to the task of reorganizing and commanding the Western cavalry, and had been promised the assistance of a few good officers from the Army of the Potomac. I had asked for Upton at the head of the list, and as soon as he was able to travel he joined me in midwinter at Gravelly Springs, Alabama, after the close of the Hood campaign. His wound was not yet entirely healed, but he at once assembled his division and set about its instruction with all his accustomed industry and enthusiasm. I have alluded to the misgivings which troubled him at the beginning of his career as a cavalry-commander, and have related how he gained the confidence of his division by his untiring devotion to their wants in camp and on the march, no less than by his conspicuous gallantry and generalship in action. The skill displayed by him in the capture of the fortifications covering Columbus by a night attack, which also resulted in the capture of nearly all the rebel troops defending them, as well as the bridges across the Chattahoochee River, thus securing for the cavalry corps a safe passage of that river into the city, and opening the way for the speedy conquest of the entire State of Georgia, has already been adverted to. This occurred on the 16th of April, 1865, and was the last considerable action of the war. It has been described by competent military critics as one of the most remarkable exploits in the history of modern cavalry. Although Upton participated in all the after-operations consequent upon the collapse of the Confederacy, including those for the capture of Jefferson Davis and the lesser rebel chiefs, as well as in the dispositions for disbanding the national army, and acquitted himself with his usual skill and ability, it may be said that the capture of Columbus closed his brilliant career as a cavalry-officer. His service in Tennessee and Kentucky and upon the Plains followed soon after, and was in turn followed by his marriage, the preparation of the infantry tactics, and the assimilation of the cavalry and artillery tactics thereto. This was the beginning of his life as a student of the art of war in its higher branches. His instruction at West Point, and his practical experience in all the arms of service for the four years of the great rebellion, had taught him all that anyone could learn of a soldier's practical duties in the field. After completing his tour as commandant of cadets at West Point, and as instructor of artillery, infantry, and cavalry tactics, he was, as before indicated, sent by the Government through Asia and Europe to study the organization, equipment, and administration of armies. Upon his return from this tour he was assigned to duty at the Artillery School of Practice as instructor of the art of war, and, while thus engaged, prepared and published the report of his observations in Europe, and began his work on the "Military Policy of the United States." During the preparation of this work he analyzed critically all the records of the Government in relation to the wars in which it had been engaged, from the beginning of the Revolution to the end of the rebellion of the slave States. The story of all this is clearly and fully set forth in the following pages, made up principally of Upton's own letters, written with the utmost freedom and unconsciousness, and, as their context shows, without the slightest expectation on his part that they would ever be collected or printed. They exhibit his character in all the stages of its moral and intellectual evolution more completely than it would be possible for any amount of description on the part of others to delineate it. And so it only remains for me to say, in

13

conclusion, as I have constantly maintained since the close of the war, that at that time Upton was as good an artillery-officer as could be found in any country, the equal of any cavalry-commander of his day, and, all things considered, was the best commander of a division of infantry in either the Union or the rebel army. He was the equal of [George Armstrong] Custer or [Judson] Kilpatrick in dash and enterprise, and vastly the superior of either in discipline and administration, whether on the march or in the camp. He was incontestably the best tactician of either army, and this is true whether tested by battle or by the evolutions of the drill-field and parade. In view of his success in all arms of the service, it is not too much to add that he could scarcely have failed as a corps or an army commander had it been his good fortune to be called to such rank. And nothing is more certain than that he would have had a corps of cavalry had the war lasted sixty days longer, or that, with the continuation of the struggle, he would have been in due time put at the head of an army. No one can read the story of his brilliant career without concluding that he had a real genius for war, together with all the theoretical and practical knowledge which anyone could acquire in regard to it. He was the equal, if not the superior, of [French General Louis Lazare] Hoche, [French General Louis] Desaix, or [Russian General Mikhail] Skobeleff, in all the military accomplishments and virtues, and up to the time when he was disabled by the disease which caused his death he was, all things considered, the most accomplished soldier in our service. His life was pure and upright, his bearing chivalric and commanding, his conduct modest and unassuming, and his character absolutely without blemish. History cannot furnish a brighter example of unselfish patriotism, or of ambition unsullied by an ignoble thought or an unworthy deed.

He was a credit to the State and family, which gave him his birth, to the Military Academy which educated him, and to the army in which he served. So long as the Union has such soldiers as he to defend it, it will be perpetual.

James Harrison Wilson.

Wilmington, Del., May s, 1885.

BOYHOOD

Emory Upton was the tenth child and sixth son of Daniel and Electa Upton, and was born on the 27th of August, 1839, in Batavia, Genesee County, New York. He was a direct descendant of John Upton, a Scotchman, the founder of the families of that name in this country.

John Upton came to America about the year 1650, and settled in Danvers, Massachusetts, then called Salem village, where his son William was born in 1663, and his grandson William in 1703. The son and grandson of the latter, both also bearing the name of William, were born in North Reading, in 1729 and 1759 respectively. The latter, removing to Dublin, New Hampshire, married Mary Morse, and the second son by this marriage was born in Dublin in 1796, and is the father of Emory, the subject of this sketch.

On his mother's side, he was descended from Stephen Randall, a native of New Hampshire. Born in Nottingham in 1782, he married Rachel Fifield, in Danville, Vermont, in 1799. On the 2d of February, 1815, after a severe wintry journey of three weeks, Mr. Randall, with his family, consisting of his wife and nine children, reached the site of a farm which he had selected in the then unbroken wilderness, near Stafford, Genesee County, New York, and, within twenty-four hours after their arrival, they were under their own shelter. With characteristic industry and prudence they not only reared a family of fourteen children, but acquired a competency, which was ever dispensed with such generosity as to make this home known far and wide as a center of hospitality.

Daniel Upton, the father of Emory, removing to New York, purchased a farm in Batavia, Genesee County, then a tract of native woods, and felled the first tree for the improvement of his homestead. On September 30, 1821, he married Electa Randall, and the young couple immediately began their married life in a log-cabin.

Members of the Methodist Protestant Church, the parents of Upton have been zealous Christians, whose lives have been consistent with their public professions of faith. Earnest believers in temperance, and stanch advocates of unfettered freedom, holding slavery to be a moral wrong, Mr. Upton never hesitated, either by word or vote, to plant himself squarely and unmistakably on the side of what he held to be right on these questions. He perceived the great value of education, and gave his children every advantage that was possible in his circumstances.

Mrs. Upton inherited a rare executive ability, sweetened by a cheerful disposition and sustained by a hopeful perseverance. A loving wife, she became the honored mother of thirteen children. Her life, necessarily a continual sacrifice, has been to her, nevertheless, full of recompense and of peace and joy. To his mother, with her abnegation of self, her untiring industry, her hopeful encouragement in the face of trials and disappointments, her tenderhearted solicitude and watchful care in the gradual unfolding of physical and mental characteristics, Emory Upton early gave testimony as the true source of all his success and honor in life. The name of mother was ever the tenderest and gentlest of words to him, for it awakened the memory of a pure and boundless love which had never failed him.

Emory Upton spent his early years upon a farm, acquiring health and strength in bodily development and the Christian influences of a pious home for the support and direction of his intellectual life.

The educational advantages enjoyed by him were such as were common to the neighborhood, supplemented by the instruction received from his elder brothers and sisters. As he approached his fifteenth year, however, his growing ambition urged him to seek the advantage of a term in college, and, with the assistance and assent of his parents, he spent the winter of 1854-55 at Oberlin College, in Ohio.

It appears, from the recollections of an intimate friend and schoolmate, that he had, at even that early day, a strong wish to enter the Military Academy at West Point, which colored his youthful life, and in some measure controlled his thoughts and actions. He was indebted to his brother James for this idea, which was speedily developed into an ardent desire for a military career by reading the life of Napoleon.

Young as he was at his first separation from home, he possessed a strong character and an independent spirit, as is clearly shown in the following narrative of a friend * who was his close companion while a student at Oberlin:

"... Whatever means he might be able to secure from home at this time, toward paying his board and tuition bills, he took a pride in not depending on it, or in calling upon home for money. He worked as many hours each day as I did. Our work was chiefly about the planing-mill and sash-factory of Mr. S. Ellis. We were paid eight cents an hour, and our work consisted for the most part in attending to the drying-kiln, filling it and emptying it, in which the poplar lumber was prepared for use in the factory. Besides this, we did any work that we could do within the hours we had allowed for that purpose. We fully agreed that no one should be ashamed of doing what ought to be done. The hours that other boys of our age spent in recreation, we spent in hard work. We scarcely took an hour's recreation in the week excepting on Sundays, when we went into the deep woods, at that time quite plenty about Oberlin, and even then we combined business with pleasure, for in the depths of the forest we read our essays to each other, or declaimed the pieces for the coming rhetorical exercises of the week. At that time, even, Emory could write well (not chirographically by any means), but his oratorical powers were defective. However, he used to console himself by saying that a soldier did not need to be an orator, for that, if he ever had to speak, it would be to his men in the face of the enemy, and on such occasions an oration must be necessarily short, and he thought he would be able for that.

"He had no taste for useless ornament in his writings, and never allowed himself to seek for frequent adjectives and high-sounding words, as young writers are wont to do; for if he were told, 'That sentence sounds poetical,' he would quietly change it to a more prosy form.

"He had no love for poets or musicians in those days. His ambition was to secure the solid basis of a practical education.

17

"His personal appearance at that time was very different from his appearance the last time I saw him. He was thin and wiry, quite freckled, his hair standing nearly straight; always in a hurry; spoke like lightning; very quick of perception, for he often cut a person off in the middle of a remark with his own reply, which was always to the point.... After our work, which was over at four o'clock in the afternoon, we went to study. We never studied the same lesson together, unless we were pushed for time, but, whenever we could, we always reviewed our lessons together just before going to class.

"He never slept on a pillow; he made his side of the bed perfectly level, and used it in this way. He was afraid of becoming round-shouldered. He would not crack a nut with his teeth, or use anything that he thought might injure them, as, he said, to have good teeth was a condition to enter West Point. We never took any part in the foolish freaks of the boys, and yet we had plenty of company in our room, and always stood good friends with our comrades.

"The great abolition movement, the underground railroad, bleeding Kansas, and all the 'isms' of that nature, were alive about this time. Emory never took any part in these demonstrations, nor spent time to hear the lectures and speeches on these subjects except, perhaps, 'Old John Brown,' and of him he did not think much. He was strongly opposed to slavery, yet he never engaged in talking about it as other young men did. More than once, on returning from rhetorical exercises, he would say: 'I am sick of such stuff. Let those fellows learn their lessons now while at school, and by-and-by, if they have any brains, they may be able to do some good.'

"We joined a literary society, but, on becoming members, we found it inclined to be an infidel affair, and at once left it. I never knew Emory Upton to use profane language, or speak with the least disrespect of religion, its ministers, or members as such. The only useless phrase he used was 'confound it.' This served all occasions. I never knew him to speak with the least levity of a woman, nor take any pleasure in jests or stories that inclined to anything disrespectful of the sex.

"Very naturally we often talked about what we should each try to be. To me it seemed almost impossible to reach my object. He had strong hopes of entering West Point, and kept that in view all the time. He frequently built large castles in the air, and, strange to say, the reality of his success as a military man surpassed in brilliancy the imagination of his youth.

"I have said that he was strongly opposed to Southern slavery. No one could be more so. At this time no one could anticipate the terrible war of the rebellion but as a possibility. He again and again felt sure that war would come. He said that he would be just ready for it. While I had no sympathy with slavery, I was not as decided an abolitionist as he was. So, on one occasion of a talk of the above nature, we agreed that, if he should be a general before he was forty-five years of age, and slavery abolished, *1 should present him with a splendid revolver, with something engraved on it to indicate the occasion and the reason why it was given. If he were not a general at that age, he should give me books to suit me, of a corresponding value. This was to be the mark or test, should we live, that as boys we could see something of the great coming events."

It so happened that at this time Judge Benjamin Pringle represented in Congress the New York district in which young Upton resided, and to him the youth owed the possession of what he so much coveted. In transmitting the letter of appointment from the Secretary of War to Upton, Judge Pringle thus advised him:

House of Representatives, Washington, D. C.,

March 12, 1856.

Dear Sir: I have the pleasure of indorsing a notice signed by the Secretary of War, informing you that the President has conditionally appointed you a cadet in the military service of the United States. I selected you for the place because, from representations made by your friends concerning you, and from my slight acquaintance with you, I believed that you possessed sufficient talent and ability, honesty and integrity, industry, energy, and perseverance to enable you to pass the ordeal at West Point creditably. Should you fail, it will be mortifying to me and to your other friends, but I trust there will be no failure. You will enter the academy under favorable circumstances, and you must make every reasonable effort to attain and maintain a high standing in your class, and if possible carry off the first honors. You can hardly imagine the interest that I feel and shall continue to feel for your success. By doing well for yourself, you will honor me. The place to which you are appointed has been sought by many and supported by influential friends, but I thought best to choose you, and you must prove to the world that I have made a good choice.

The first step toward the realization of his ambition had been taken, and, intermingled with the great happiness that almost overwhelmed the young appointee, there was an ever-present determination, stronger even than his joy, that nothing should be left undone on his part to show to Judge Pringle that he would prove worthy of his favor. Never in his after honorable career did he forget the debt he owed the judge, and in his times of marked success he constantly reiterated, "I owe all to Judge Pringle." Loyalty and gratitude were henceforth prominent among his other good qualities. Every spare hour (and he ordinarily rose those wintry mornings before five o'clock), after the reception of the above letter, was devoted to his studies, that he might not fail on his entrance examination, and with such success that, on the 1st of July, 1856, he was admitted a conditional cadet into the Military Academy at West Point.

In considering the influences that so far had molded this as yet uneventful life, there are some traits that may be specially designated. As a boy he was conscientious, for he did his duty willingly, cheerfully, and thoroughly before he sought the pleasures of play and recreation; he was pure in heart, clean of speech, and took no delight in coarse jests or idle words; and, above all, he was greatly in earnest in whatever he undertook, and thus he accomplished more than he had hoped.

CADET-LIFE AT WEST POINT

Upton reported at West Point on the 3d of June, 1856, and it was soon evident that he came with a firm determination to meet manfully all difficulties, and to "become a general before he was forty-five years of age."

By the 20th of June there were gathered together from all sections of the country about one hundred young men on the same errand, selected, for one reason or another, by their respective Congressmen as fit to enter upon military life. It is an instructive sight, and one calculated to give rise to many emotions, to look upon the earnest countenances of these youths. For the time being they may be taken as the truest outcome of our people, representing, in their undeveloped powers, the immediate future generation of our country, as the members of Congress represent the present. The dress, appearance, stature, dialect, culture, and material condition of the various sections of the country, are here well exhibited, not as the best but rather as the average. But, after the young men have passed through their elementary drill, and are uniformed, the barriers due to differences of previous condition are soon broken down, and those elements of humanity that unite us to our friends and associates prove stronger than the accidents of birth, or the influences of wealth or station. Like seek like: the manly and generous join in comradeship; the weak and trifling are mingled but not united; the vicious seek strength in union, and so the several strata are arranged. The strongest associations are at first those of classmates, but in later years these include members of other classes. The deprivations, hardships, and sacrifices of the military service cement these friendly associations in after-life into the love and affection of a great brotherhood.

Upton was exceptionally well-equipped for the new life upon which he was now about to enter. With high principles, and the courage to defend them when the occasion was pressing, he possessed the modest demeanor of true worth. At first, he suffered under the imputation of a lack of courage from his quiet and unassuming behavior; in the end, his comrades discovered that they

21

had mistaken his character. None suspected, underneath the modest bearing, the existence of the high purpose to which he had devoted his whole heart. He perfectly understood that before he could receive the diploma of the institution, and his commission as an officer of the army, work would have to be done, so great in its importance to him that, to accomplish it well, he would need the steadiest application of his time, the severest study, and the concentration of all his physical and mental powers. It is also worthy of note that he—a youth of sixteen—clearly foresaw the danger which threatened the Union, and actively sought to fit himself most thoroughly to aid in its preservation.

Making due allowances for the impetuosity of youth, the following extracts from his letters to his sister Maria [one year his senior] give a reasonably true exhibit of the influence of West Point training in the formation of our embryo soldier; and, in passing, we must not fail to estimate at its true value the effect of this sister's love, which, alive to his needs, cultivated with its womanly power the nobler qualities of her brother, and with its clear intuition guided and directed him in his new career. Let these letters, then, written in the freshness of youth and with the generous confidence of boyhood, tell the story of his cadet-life:

February 25, 1857.

Dear Sister:... I am glad to hear of your good health and assiduity to study, and that you are exerting every faculty in the laudable pursuit of education. I am striving equally hard for the same. I am sure that few have the facilities offered for getting an education which I have, and not to take advantage of these privileges is inconsistent. I study from 6 to 7 a. m., and from 8 a. m. to 1 p. m., including recitations; then from 2 to 4 p. m. I read newspapers and write letters; from 4 p. m. till sundown is release from quarters, which I usually spend in the library reading, and then study from 7 to 9.30 p. m.; so that you see my time is pretty well occupied. Perhaps a few of my daily marks would give you an idea of my progress.... So long as I can keep up to these marks I am not in danger of being found deficient.... I am passionately attached to West Point, and would not give up my appointment here for a million dollars. I want you to come here next encampment and see the beautiful scenery that I have often tried to describe.

My DEAR Sister:... In your last letter you asked if I sincerely believed in a God. I can say yes. I also believe in the religion inculcated by the ministers of God.... Few men now disbelieve religion, and those are mostly ignorant men. Voltaire, the greatest modern infidel, shrank from death; and why? Because of his unbelief. He was afraid to enter eternity. I hope that you will never desert the good cause you have espoused, and that you will do much good in your life. As for myself, I take the Bible as the standard of morality, and try to read two chapters in it daily.

West Point, September 7, 1857.

My dear Sister:... In your letter you allude to my demerit. I must say that it gave me the bluest kind of blues; not because it made me have any apprehension of being "found," but because you look upon them in a wrong light. Now, I'll disabuse you of this error. You use the term "bad marks." Bad signifies to you, evil, wrong, immoral, and wicked, which placed before marks signifies that I have been doing something wrong or immoral—something which conscience disapproves. That is wrong, not only in the sight of a military man, but of God. Now, what moral wrong is there in "laughing in ranks," in being "late at roll-call," "not stepping off at command," "not having coat buttoned throughout," and kindred reports? Now, is that wrong in the sight of God? I say, no! But it is wrong only in the sight of a military man, and it is from such reports that I get my demerits or "bad-marks." I can say I have never received an immoral report, such as "using profane language." I thank you for the kind admonition, and to please you I will try to get as few as possible. I have only one so far this month, and if I get no more that will come off. I certainly shall be careful enough to prevent being cut a single day on furlough.

West Point, February 13, 1858.

Dear Sister:... I received a letter from Sister L—, in which she says that she and S— have experienced religion. I hope they may have the strength to defend and exemplify it throughout their whole lives. I also hope they have attained it through a firm conviction of its being right, and that the irresistible current of a protracted meeting did not hasten them to take such an important step. Do not infer from this that I am opposed to such meetings, for I am not; on the contrary, I think they cause two thirds of the true conversions, but you know that young and inconsiderate persons often catch the enthusiasm of an excited minister, and believe they have found religion; but, as soon as the meetings cease, their enthusiasm subsides, from the want of thorough conviction, and they necessarily revert to their primitive state. My reason for not seeking religion can only be ascribed to a queer kind of apathy.

West Point, February 9, 1859.

My dear Sister:... The perusal of your last letter gave me great pain, yet I am glad you gave me so clear an insight into brother Le Roy's disease. I have but little hope of his recovery, and I only ask that he may be prepared for his last great change. Oh, that I could by look, word, or deed, ease his condition, but I can only think of and pity him! My last thoughts at night and my first waking thoughts are of him. How I wish I was at home, to watch by him and contribute my mite toward comforting him! May he not delay in making his peace with God! How thankful I am for such parents as we have! Their sacred influence is ever about us, shielding us from temptation, and teaching us the true object of life. If Le Roy cannot get well, I wish to be sent for; I cannot part with him forever without a last farewell.

West Point, March 26, 1859.

Dear Sister:... Dear Le Roy's request to me shall not be unheeded. I have resolved, yes, begun to seek the Lord, and shall continue till I find him. "He is slow to anger and of great kindness." Relying on the promise that "whosoever will seek mercy shall obtain it," I will leave no effort untried, but will work diligently to the end....

West Point, April 23, 1859.

Dear Sister:... You have doubtless heard that I have put my trust in the "Friend that sticketh closer than a brother." Such is my hope. Life is but an instant as compared with eternity, and, when we reflect that our future condition depends upon our actions here in this world, it is but reasonable that we should bow before the Creator, to acknowledge his supremacy and ask his forgiveness for our manifold violations of his law. I feel that I could resign everything to do his will and to gain his approbation. today being Easter, the Lord's Supper will be celebrated. I intend to partake of it willingly, and hope that I may be strengthened in my resolutions to serve him faithfully to the end. The army is a hard place to practice religion; though few scoff at it, yet a great majority totally disregard it. Still, through the prayers of others I hope to lead a Christian life, and to do as much good in the army as in

24

any other profession. I do not think that Christians have ever disgraced the profession of arms; on the contrary, they are those who have most ennobled it.

West Point, May 1, 1859.

Dear Cousin E—: I have heard that you have experienced a change of heart, and that you propose to live hereafter a Christian life. This gives me great joy. I, too, have given myself up to God. Being, therefore, new laborers in the vineyard of the Lord, I thought that a correspondence might mutually benefit and strengthen us in the determination we have made. I do sincerely hope that you have "offered yourself as a sacrifice, holy and acceptable before the Lord," and have a hope of immortality. What a blessed thought! Is it not a sufficient inducement to remain faithful to the end? Yes! what is the length of life, compared with never-ending eternity? Infinitely small. Yet our actions during this instant are to determine our future condition throughout eternity. Let us strive to show ourselves worthy of the kingdom of heaven. Let us be true to the trust confided in us. We must necessarily encounter difficulties. We gray have to bear the scoffs of the world, but we should recollect that the Son of God not only had to bear this, but he was crucified, and his blood was shed for us. Doubts may arise in our minds; but we must remember that we are finite beings, and God is infinite. How, therefore, can we expect to comprehend the ways of an Infinite Being? Let us drop these doubts whenever they arise, and hope and trust in God, "who is just and merciful, slow to anger, and of great kindness." The more difficulties we triumph over, the greater will be our reward. Let us not, therefore, be discouraged or disheartened, but may we grow in the knowledge and love of God, that we may finally be accounted worthy of a seat at his right hand.

West Point, January 6, 1860.

My dear Sister: Another year has joined the past, and 1860, bright with promises, has dawned upon us. "We know not what a day may bring forth." 1860 may be as indelibly stamped upon our memories as 1859 or 1856, when our loved ones were summoned from earth. As we look over our diminished numbers, we ask who is to go next. The one most robust in health may be the first to succumb to disease. Let us thank God for his goodness and mercy, for we feel that he has called them unto his glory. We should be more watchful, more diligent in our services to God than we have been. Let our united prayers ascend to

God that he may hasten the conversion of those of our family who still delay.

West Point, January 20, 1860.

My dear Sister:... The nature of your letter shows conclusively your deep interest in my welfare. Your letter did me much good. In order to answer its questions, I had to examine myself to ascertain what motives actuate me. I cannot be too thankful for having been reared under Christian influences, for especially at this time do I need the assistance of God to keep me in the path of rectitude. We are living in perilous times. Government, society, everything seem to be on the verge of revolution. The passions of the people are being waked up, and they must have vent. God is directing the storm, and all is for the best. We may ask, How have we incurred his displeasure? The answer is easy. Mormonism, spiritualism, intemperance, slavery, corruption in politics, either of which is almost sufficient to curse a people. Few there are who have not bowed the knee to Baal. We must have reform. We must return to reason and virtue. Why should we expect tolerance when God suffered such calamities to befall his own chosen people? He scourged them with war, and he will punish us likewise. If we are to have war, I shall have no conscientious scruples as to engaging in it, for I believe I shall be on the side of right. I am ambitious; but I shall strive to limit it to doing good. It will profit a man nothing to gain the whole world and lose his own soul. Since I first began to call upon God, I have daily asked his assistance and direction, and I feel that he is nearer me now than ever before. You know not to what temptations we are exposed here, yet he has not allowed me to be tempted further than I could bear. Whenever lethargy, indifference, or skepticism has crept over me, the remembrance that our sister and brother died happy, trusting in God, has been an incentive to renewed effort to continue faithful to the end. I shall trust in God. If he intends me to occupy a high position, he will raise me to it; if not, I shall be happy in having done my duty and in meeting his approval. There will be no limit to the opportunities of doing good in the army. There will be wounded soldiers to minister to, and the dying to comfort. Surely I can do good. These remarks may be premature; but the conviction strengthens that we must have war. I thank God that none of my relatives will feel its horrors; but I pity those where the conflict must occur.

From the perusal of these letters we see that the loss of a beloved younger brother [Le Roy] directed Upton's thoughts toward the future life. And, while his sister's letters kept him fully informed, of the incidents of home-life, they also encouraged the growing interest in his soul's welfare.

He had passed through the troubles of his first encampment, had learned to yield unquestioned obedience to his superior officers, had mastered all the studies preceding those of the professional year, and had measured himself with his comrades in the soldierly and intellectual race. As he had risen gradually in class-standing through his own merits, there became established in his mind a confidence in his own powers that removed from him any fear of ultimate failure. The regular habits enforced by the discipline of the academy had put his bodily functions in systematic working order and given him perfect health. His religious feelings were not, therefore, tinctured with the morbid fancies arising from ill-health in body or mind, but were really the awakenings of his moral manhood to the necessity of a dependence upon his heavenly Father. These religious seeds, first planted by his parents, and nurtured by his sister, took firm root in his nature, and afterward developed into a healthy growth, commensurate with the necessities of his after-life.

He had escaped the dangers of that period of his youth when the rational faculties are first strongly developed and often run in wanton riot, their whole effect being too often to submerge the intellect in the bogs and quicksands of materialism. Ever after, Upton was a deeply religious man in principle, in thought, and in action, and the evidences of this fact are readily traced throughout his subsequent career in all his words and deeds.

His cadet comrades knew him to be a member of the church, of the Bible-class, and prayer-meeting, and they gave him the credit of being conscientiously consistent in profession and in life. While this consistency exacted and obtained their respect and support, it also diverted from him the sneers and innuendoes which might be occasionally directed against less worthy and less consistent comrades.

Up to this time Upton had secured the reputation of being a reliable but not a brilliant scholar. A laborious student, faithfully doing his day's work in the day, he managed to exhibit in his recitations always a good knowledge of the subject-matter, but his early deficiency of expression even here prevented his ever making a thoroughly well-rounded and elegant recitation. What he learned, however, he retained, and constantly gave practical value to his knowledge by using illustrative facts to fix theoretical principles in his mind. His mathematical training caused him to prove all things, to take nothing for granted, and pass, by consecutive logical processes, to the inevitable result. During this last year at the academy he was constantly looking forward to the time of his emancipation, not because of ennui or mental fatigue, but rather because the practical application of principles was becoming a necessity to him. Mixed with these longings were the occasional retrospective glances in which the young frequently indulge. A few letters are here inserted to exhibit this phase of his student-life:

West Point, February 5, 1860.

My dear Sister:... I have just been discussing with my room-mate our prospects as army-officers. My life really begins with the date of my commission. What will time disclose? I may meet with success, and I may have been educated but to become the mark of a "red-skin." Our profession differs from all others. It is a profession of fate and a fatal profession. A long war would make many of us, and prove the grave of as many; but you know it matters not how we meet death, provided we are prepared for it. We must leave all to the dispensation of an all-wise Providence.

West Point, June 3, 1860.

My dear Sister:... This is the anniversary of my arrival at West Point. Four years ago today, in the pride and buoyant spirits of a young military aspirant, I took my first lessons in military life. 'Tis pleasant to look back upon the past and compare it with the present. Four years of constant confinement and regular duties have passed, and we now stand on the threshold of our first class-year. Hard times and troubles are all over, and inviting scenes lie before us. One short year more, and the key which is to unlock the honors and emoluments of our profession will be delivered into our hands. I hope to do well, since my general standing in a great degree will depend on my examination. Chemistry, infantry, artillery, and cavalry tactics will follow the examination in ethics. Were it not for drawing, I should, without doubt, better my last year's standing. I shall probably not fall below it.

The Secretary of War has decided not to grant us a leave. My only plea is a broken shoulder, got in the riding-hall, but, as I am getting "painfully smart," my hopes, even in that direction, are diminutive. You may, therefore, regard my leave as extremely doubtful, and even dis- miss it from your mind. I am very sorry to disappoint my loved ones.

West Point, October 21, 1860.

My dear Sister: The Prince of Wales [Albert Edward, eldest son of Queen Victoria] created a good deal of excitement here on Monday last. The plain was thronged with people eager to get a glimpse of the future King of England [ascended 1901 as Edward VII]. We were drawn up in line in front of barracks to receive the prince. He and his suite were mounted and preceded by a platoon of dragoons, as escort. As he came galloping along the line we came to "present arms." I never experienced such queer feelings before, and, had I not been under military discipline, I believe my enthusiasm would have given vent to itself in cheers. The crowd was wild, but was doubtless somewhat restrained by the example of the corps. After the review, the officers of my class were introduced to his Royal Highness. I can now say that my rustic hand has grasped the hand of royalty. He has a kind and very pleasant countenance, and he will probably make a good if not a brilliant sovereign. The members of his suite are perfect gentlemen (General Bruce, Duke of Newcastle, Dr. Ackland, and others). They came into the engineering-rooms and I had quite an interesting conversation with them. They spoke pure English. We rode before them in the riding-hall with saddles, and then with blankets. One cadet was thrown almost off his horse, but he regained his seat with such skill and address as to make the prince clap his hands. After the ride, the prince expressed his admiration of our horsemanship to the officer in command....

Bishop McIlvaine, of Ohio, preached us a sermon last Sunday. He was chaplain here thirty years ago, and during his ministry a great revival took place. He attended our prayer-meeting and commenced to relate his experience here, but, unfortunately, his interesting narrative was interrupted by the 'call to quarters.' West Point was then a hot-bed of infidelity, but he rooted it out, and his influence is felt to this day. I was introduced to him, and he gave me a warm invitation to visit him at Cincinnati next year. Please give me credit for not saying anything about my studies in this letter.

29

West Point, October 28, 1860.

My dear little Sister: Your letter was duly received; and, as it was full of information, it was read with no ordinary degree of satisfaction. You alone of the thirteen children remain at home. What a change! One by one they have left the paternal roof, until you only are left "to honor thy parents." None of us can reproach our father and mother for neglect of duty. I can now appreciate the effect of the discipline under which we were trained. Rigid though it was at times, yet the chastisement was always given in love rather than in anger. Our characters were formed early; and, hence, none of us when thrown upon our own resources have thus far disgraced our name. You are now my only home correspondent, and you must write all that transpires at home. Every letter you write has two values, one to yourself and one to the recipient; therefore think not that your letters are worthless; they help to develop your mental faculties.... Education is not wholly acquired in the school-room. Accomplishments must result from mingling in society. Education and politeness make the accomplished lady. You will soon be sent away to school, but bear in mind that you can improve out of school. Every day, by close observation, you can discern more and more what is your duty. Observe the actions of others, but do so without evincing curiosity, for that were rude.

From this time until near the close of Upton's cadet-life, the great questions which agitated political parties throughout the whole land, and excited the animosities of the people, had their influence among the cadets. Intimately associated by the ties of home and kindred with all parts of our country, West Point exhibited in miniature the varying phases of sectional differences and of irreconcilable grievances. Brother cadets who had endured the same hardships, had exchanged the warmest and dearest confidences, had studied and roomed together, began now to have wordy warfare, to foster animosities, and to look askance at each other. A segregation of the opposing elements took place; and, while there were many who, animated by the fire and zeal of their section, were ready to urge extreme measures, nearly all of the Southern cadets felt that the hour of separation, which was to tear them away from dearly loved friends and their beloved West Point, was steadily but surely approaching, and that no man's hand was strong enough to prevent.

Many left with great sorrow and reluctance. Some that hesitated, torn by the conflicting emotions of duty and love, and of stern necessity, were hurried by a fate as inexorable as history records. All left with a sorrow so great that manly tears dropped silently as they bade farewell to their comrades—now friends, but soon to be foes. As a type of the influences at work in the hearts and minds of these young men on both sides, so differently reared in political thought and belief, and called upon to make choice, when apparently the foundations of government were being shaken to their center, the letters of Upton will exhibit an interesting picture. At this time, as well as for several years previous, the cadets had by some gradual process become separated into two parties, hostile in sentiment and even divided in barracks. This building of granite was separated really into two parts by the sally-port, and the cadets of Northern or Union principles lived mainly in the east wing, while the Southerners occupied the west and south wings. On Washington's birthday in 1861, when the band played the national airs at reveille, the hisses of the secessionists called forth the cheers of the Union men and roused them into a condition of active personal hostility. From that moment the lines were sharply drawn, and, while not actually coming to open breaches of the peace, the segregation became complete. The Northern spirit, difficult to arouse, was tempered like steel, and the smallest incident served to bring the opposing principles into actual conflict. Little by little, however, the strength of the Southern wing diminished by resignation, until the few who were left contented themselves with silent endurance until all were finally eliminated.

West Point, December 1, 1860.

My dear Sister: You must pardon me, but I must introduce the general and all-absorbing topic of conversation—secession. What do people at home think of it? I believe the Union is virtually dissolved. South Carolina cannot retract. Her honor demands that she secede, else she would be a "by-word." But secession is revolution. She will seize Fort Moultrie, and hence a collision with the General Government must follow. War would alienate all the other Southern States from the Union, and a terrible and bloody revolution will result. Everyone in South Carolina is for disunion, at least none dare avow themselves for the Union, and from the accounts in the New York daily papers I sincerely believe she will secede on the 18th or 19th of this month. If so, the North and the South will be speedily arrayed against each other, and the result will be that the North will be victorious. The South Carolina cadets published a manifesto a short time since as follows:

"West Point, November 9, 1860.

"To the Editor of the *Columbia (S. C.) Guardian.*

"Mr. Editor—Sir: From what we have seen and heard, South Carolina will undoubtedly, at an early period, redeem her assertions, take her destinies in her own hands, and proceed at once to organize for herself a new and separate government (a government of which our beloved Calhoun would approve were he with us at this time), one in which the benefits are equally distributed to all.

"Now we, her sons and representatives at the United States Military Academy at West Point, are eager to manifest our devotion and affection to her and her present cause; so will we, simultaneously with her withdrawal, be found under the folds of her banner, fighting for liberty or equality.

"Though the reception of a diploma here at the National Academy is certainly to be desired by all of us, yet we cannot so stifle our convictions of duty as to serve the remainder of our time here under such a man as Mr. Lincoln as commander-in-chief, and to be subjected at all times to the orders of a government the administration of which must be necessarily unfriendly to the Commonwealth which has so far preserved a spotless record, and of which we are justly proud.

"We hereby swear to be true to her lone star in the present path of rectitude; and if, by chance, she goes astray, we will be with her still. All we desire is a field for making ourselves useful."

A Philadelphia paper exposed their class standing here. "Three were deficient at the examination, one ranked fifty-three out of a class of fifty-seven, and the remaining three had not appeared in the Register of Cadets." I will state that two of the latter will be "found" this January examination, one was recently placed in arrest for an offense equivalent to forgery, and which would dismiss him if brought before a court-martial. Three have resigned (one left today), and the others will probably follow soon.

If the worst is to come and war follow, I am ready. I will take for my motto, *Dieu et mon droit*. I will strive to do my full duty to God and my country, and willingly abide the consequences. I thank Fortune for having been given a military education here, and I will make myself useful. Always remember me to Judge Pringle. You know not under what obligations I feel to him. All my success in life I shall owe to him. I forbear writing more at present, and will await future developments.

West Point, December 21, 1860.

Dear Sister: We are on general review in mineralogy and geology preparatory to our last January examination, and, possibly, our very last. These are delightful studies, and the method of instruction here renders us very familiar with minerals. Each rock has now its story for us.... The political horizon is very black. today's papers inform us that South Carolina has seceded. The veil behind which Webster sought not to penetrate has been "rent in twain," and secession, with its evils, is now a reality. Let her go. She has been a pest, an eye-sore, an abomination ever since she entered the Union. Were it not that her example may become contagious, few would regret her course; but, in the present excited state of feeling at the South, there is imminent danger that the whole South will drift into the terrible gulf which secession opens before them. I believe in Union, but South Carolina has taken the initiative, and she is responsible for whatever follows, and posterity will hold her so. Every friend of freedom will execrate her course. War, I believe, must speedily follow, and by her act. The papers say, "Buchanan has ordered the commandant of Fort Moultrie to surrender if attacked"; if true, what a traitor! Floyd has sent twenty-five thousand stand of arms to different Southern posts within the past year, and for what? Certainly not for the use of soldiers garrisoning them. What, then, is the inference? That they shall be convenient for secession. The Administration must be deeply implicated in this plot to destroy the government. Its conduct cannot be explained otherwise. I heartily rejoice that Abraham Lincoln is elected, and that we have such a noble set of Republicans at Washington to meet this critical emergency. As for myself, I am ambitious, and desire fame, but I will stand by the right; for what is the worth of fame when purchased by dishonor? God orders or suffers all things.

West Point, January 12, 1861.

My dear Sister: This is examination-week. My reports have not been quite so good as you may have desired, but I shall be quite satisfied

33

with the results of the examinations.... Truly troublous times are upon us. We are at sea, with no chart to guide us. What the end will be, our wisest statesmen cannot foresee. The South is gone, and the question is, Will the Government coerce her back? The attempt, I think, will be made, but we cannot predict the result. Southern men are brave, and will fight well, but their means for prosecuting a long war are wanting. Four States are now out of the Union, and South Carolina has fired the first gun. She has resisted the entrance of the Star of the West to Fort Sumter, and, no doubt, there will be bloodshed before you receive this, since the *Brooklyn* (man-of-war) is on the way to Charleston, and is bound to re-enforce that fort.... Members of my class continue to resign. The corps is already sensibly reduced in numbers, and, from present prospects, we will almost be reduced to a moiety. Should the United States officers from the seceding States resign, there will be many vacancies, and, very probably, they would be filled by graduating us soon.... In my next letter I will try to say nothing upon secession, but it is the absorbing topic of thought at present.

West Point, February 2, 1861.

My dear Brother: I have not heard from you in a long time. I want to ascertain your views on the subject of secession. It has assumed immense importance. The crisis has come. How is it to be met? The Union is in extreme peril. Must it be dissolved? No! I say, let it be preserved, if it costs years of civil war. What do you think of compromise? I am opposed to it, as a dangerous precedent. If the Union could be preserved without compromise, even at the expense of a war, I think it would be preferable to a compromise, since it would demonstrate that a republican government is adequate to any emergency. But, rather than see the country forever disrupted, I would prefer an honorable adjustment. These views I take on the supposition that the South feels herself aggrieved, and that she desires to perpetuate the Union, if possible. Northern aggression is the alleged, not the real, cause of secession. The Legislature of South Carolina declares she will not remain in the Union under any circumstances. They are wild on the subject of a Southern confederacy, and they have resolved to establish it at the price of a revolution. If this is the real cause of secession, the door to compromise should forever be closed, and the South should be completely subjugated. In the Union, their property is and ought to be protected; out of the Union, slavery is overthrown. I hope someday to see it abolished peaceably; but, if they go out, they of themselves overthrow it in blood. It is a great evil, but

34

we are not responsible. Let them answer for and settle it themselves. I believe that.an all-wise Providence is directing the storm, and that he will overrule everything for good.... Several Southern cadets left today, and many more will follow soon. Promotion will be rapid in the army about the time we graduate, and if there is a war we will not lack employment. Probably an assault will be made on Fort Sumter; they will meet with a warm reception. We are on our last term. Our studies—military engineering, law, ordnance, etc.—are very interesting and we look forward with great pleasure to our graduation.

West Point, March 27, 1861.

Dear Sister: Your remarks upon "Tories" were very appropriate. There is a large class at the North, and they will seriously affect the power of the Government. They are so servile that they would prefer to accept the terms of Jeff Davis, rather than fight for the honor of the North. I am entirely out of patience with them. Let slavery alone where it is, but never let it extend. Think of a slave republic in the nineteenth century! The ignorant people of Italy are now fighting for liberty; the chivalrous South is fighting for slavery. What a cause to fight for; and still Northern traitors are taking commissions in the Southern army! It is good for the army that they have resigned; they are now in their proper places. It is no compliment to the cause to say that traitors are eager to defend it. I am impatient with the apathy of the North. The South is making ample preparations for war, while we "are lying supinely on our backs." Why are no steps taken to defend the Union? If we have war (mark my words), Jeff Davis will be successful in one or two campaigns. He is energetic, and he is drawing all the talent he can from our army. He will enter the war with his forces well organized, and it cannot be denied that Southern men will fight well; hence, what is to prevent his success for a time? Every victory for him at the outset will require three defeats to offset.

West Point, April 8, 1861.

My dear Sister:... I am sincerely glad at the turn affairs have taken within the last few days. The Government has awakened from its apparent lethargy, and seems disposed to meet the difficulties with which it is beset. Unwonted activity is displayed at army rendezvous and at navy-yards.

My opinion is that war has actually begun. There is absence of news from Charleston. The telegraph lines are down south of Petersburg, Virginia, which is a very suspicious circumstance. The gallant band at

Fort Sumter may now be sacrificing their lives in defense of our flag and for the honor of our country. This sacrifice will not be in vain. The acts of the Government are decidedly warlike, but not aggressive. Southern troops are assembling at Forts Pickens and Sumter; this all means war; it cannot be evaded. Traitorous army officers are resigning daily. Let them go; we want none but faithful men. I am glad to say that almost every Northern cadet is anxious and ready to serve the Government. War is a calamity, but an inevitable necessity. I think there will be a campaign this summer, else secession must back clean down, which is improbable.... A letter was, received today from Washington, stating that the Secretary of War and General Scott are in favor of graduating our class, and giving us commissions to fill vacancies now existing in the army. I am willing to be ordered away immediately. A furlough would give little satisfaction when such exciting scenes are being daily enacted. I shall be glad when my academic duties terminate.

West Point, April 8, 1861.

My very dear Sister: You will, before the reception of this, have heard the war news. The daily papers teem with exciting dispatches. Troops are moving in every direction. All, however, is speculation as to their destination and orders. I rejoice that the Government has taken its stand.

Let it pursue a firm policy, and I am sure the North will support it. An attack on Fort Sumter is highly probable. The "Times" and "Herald" today state that provisions are on their way there, and that Anderson has orders to open his batteries if the vessel is fired upon. I hope Providence is overruling us, and that all will turn out for the best. The war will be forced upon us. We will be in the right, and let us maintain it as becomes freemen.

I mentioned in my last letter that we might graduate soon. I hope we may if war begins. I want no holier cause than to defend the flag which Washington honored. Will you do me the favor to make a little flag (inclosed size), with thirteen stripes and thirty-four stars? I want it for my personal colors, to have always with me. With that, a small pocket Testament, and a just cause, I am ready for action, and willing to leave the issue in the hands of God. I shall hope to see you soon, whatever transpires. You must see West Point. I am having a very easy time—no military duty to perform, no roll-calls to attend, etc.—these are privileges of the office I now hold, Assistant Instructor of Artillery.

Remember me most kindly to Judge Pringle. I owe all to him. His motive in appointing me seldom actuates other Congressmen. Most appointments are political favors. I told you the reason he assigned for appointing me.

West Point, April 17, 1861.

My very dear Sister: Your very welcome letter was received today. I admire the feelings which dictated it. I rejoice that you are all willing that I should serve my country. That I should witness the worst horrors of war very soon, admits of no doubt, but I do not shrink from it. I shall have the pleasing and grateful knowledge that, every morning and evening, prayers will ascend for my protection and spiritual welfare.... I am both surprised and delighted at the enthusiasm of the people in support of the Government. Every breath of treason in the North seems hushed. How remarkable! One week ago, no one had any confidence. today, the voice is, "The Union must and shall be preserved!" The attack on Fort Sumter has sealed the traitors' doom.

Now for the "petit" flag. It is suspended over my alcove, where I can look at it by turning my eye. I shall carry it with me during the war in my breast-pocket. I shall look at it whenever necessary to stimulate my sense of duty, and I shall look at it often to call you into remembrance. I am much pleased with the letters I receive from every member of our family. All tell me to do my duty, and none would dissuade me. Nothing encourages me more, and I would like to have duty inculcated in every letter. I shall not have a furlough, and it is doubtful even if I return home for an hour. For mother's sake, I believe it is better that I should not. Thirty members of my class have applied to the Secretary of War to be graduated at once. The remainder (eighteen) are doubtful, and some are traitors. They refused to sign the paper. The application has been laid before the superintendent.... The Government will know who are loyal and who are traitors. I think the latter will not get diplomas; if they do graduate, I believe they will immediately join the C. S. A.; one already holds a commission. Union meetings are held here almost every night. All the national airs, except "Hail Columbia," are sung. Cheers for the Union are loud and long. We are strong for the Union, now and forever.

We may now cast a retrospective glance over the past five years, and determine the influences which the Academy had planted, fostered, and developed in Upton's mental, moral, and physical nature. We find him, at his entrance into cadet-life, a raw country lad, with few of the graces and but little of the polish that mark the youth trained amid the elegancies of city life. But, deeply ingrained in his moral nature, there were fixed principles of integrity, devotion to duty, and filial and fraternal love, cemented by the powerful, ever-inciting activities of a religious mind. Thrown into a community where unquestioned obedience was at once required, discontent and active resistance would have unquestionably followed, had not the logic of its necessity soon found a lodgment and a hearty acceptance in his mind. A unit in an organization governed by a system of regulations, whose direct results confirmed its wisdom, he soon gave his adhesion and support to the constituted authorities; for, just as soon as he began to appreciate the fallacy of his reasoning as to the moral wrong of "bad marks," these decreased in due proportion.

The regulations established for the government of the cadets are explicit, and are devised to train them into systematic and regular habits. Violations of regulations are followed by restrictions, which are wisely corrective in their nature and not punitive. The immediate administration in quarters, at drill, and in military evolutions of all kinds, while supervised by army officers, is mainly confided to cadets who are judged by their comrades according to the impartial standards of equity and right in the performance of their duty. This instills a respect for authority, independent of the individual exercising it for the time being, leads to an honorable rivalry for the coveted honors, and confers on the governors and governed the sense of personal responsibility, which is essentially the pride and glory of the Academy. The daily exaction of many hours of hard study, cheerfully yielded by the cadet because of the impartial benefits received, results in a continuous growth of mental fiber and develops a self-reliance which finds its highest value in times of necessity, responsibility, or peril.

And, finally, of higher value than all else, is the true soldierly honor which, ever jealously guarding the priceless jewel of truth, requires the sacrifice of life itself before the trust shall be betrayed or the flag dishonored. This devotion to truth guarantees to each member of the Academy a reliance on his word as an officer and a gentleman, and demands of him such conduct as shall be the manly outcome of noble and patriotic thoughts.

Such was the atmosphere which had surrounded Upton during his cadetship at West Point. It was one well calculated to nourish and invigorate his moral growth, and to destroy the very germs of selfish actions. The system of responsibility toward his superiors, and the exercise of his power in his relation to his subordinates, happily balanced in their influence, led him to acquire a proper respect for authority, and a just discretion in its exercise. His intellect, quickened by the daily study, grew in due proportion with the manly vigor acquired from his physical exercise, and thus we find him well equipped at all points for the important duties which his chosen profession of necessity called him to perform amid the stern realities of war.

Under the orders of Confederate General P.G.T. Beauregard, Fort Sumter was fired upon on April 12, 1861.—Ed. 2016

His class graduated on the 6th of May, 1861. His academic rank was eight in a class of forty-five members. The Academic Board considered him fit to be honored by recommendation to the Secretary of War for promotion into the Engineers and all other corps and line of the army. He had, therefore, justified the high expectations of his friend Judge Pringle, for he had reached the highest honor the Academy had to bestow. Notwithstanding this recommendation, he chose the artillery. With his comrades he was ordered to report without delay at Washington, where their services were sorely needed to drill and discipline the various regiments of volunteer troops gathered there in obedience to the call of the Government, preparatory to the arduous campaign then in contemplation.

ACTIVE SERVICE AS A SUBALTERN

The great body of volunteers assembled at Washington in the spring of 1861, in obedience to the call of the President, although inspired by patriotic enthusiasm, was without discipline or military knowledge, save the little they had individually acquired by their service in the militia. To remedy these defects became, then, a matter of pressing necessity before the troops could with confidence be sent into the field. The War Department, doubtless with this end in view, ordered the graduation of the two upper classes of the Military Academy, in order to utilize the services of these carefully trained and thoroughly disciplined young men in drilling the various regiments of volunteers. Upton's class was graduated on the 6th of May, and had completed all but a month of their five years' cadet service. They were in every way qualified for the responsible duties to which they were at once assigned. Imperative orders directed their immediate presence in Washington. Delaying but a few hours in New York to procure their arms and equipments for active service, many of them still in their cadet uniform, they hurried on to Washington, and were at once absorbed in the performance of the duty assigned them.

Coming as they did fresh from the Military Academy, accustomed to strict disciplinary principles, having a practical as well as a theoretical knowledge of military science, and with a high sense of honor, they were peculiarly fortunate in being at once associated with those patriotic men who formed the first levy of our volunteer army.

They could not help being ennobled by intimate association with the men who, in the highest spirit of self-sacrifice, had given up every worldly interest, as well as family and home, and who stood ready to yield life itself in order that the Union might be preserved.

The influence of such men upon these active and high-spirited young regulars can never be wholly understood, except in the light of the remarkable success that the latter attained by the hearty cooperation of the former; and the regular army of today shows that the patriotic and devoted sacrifice of our volunteer soldiery has had an absorbing influence upon its present temper and discipline.

The complete story of the great civil war can never be fully written until the faithful historian has, by careful study and patient effort, constructed the mosaic from the tiny bits of personal and official experience scattered here and there in almost inextricable confusion. Each individual actor in the great conflict has his part to play, and his story has its place in the completed picture.

Upton was a faithful correspondent, and the letters to his relatives kept them well informed of his movements, and of the events which came under his immediate notice.

In the delineation of his character, it is sufficient for our purpose to give copious extracts from his letters, believing that these were the true expression of his thoughts, motives, and actions, at the time of writing, and this is our excuse for using his own words in telling the story of his life.

Washington, D. C., May 8, 1861.

My dear Sister: From New York we took the 6 p. m. train for Philadelphia. Everything passed off quietly until we arrived in the City of Brotherly Love. There we were met by a strong police force, and all were arrested for secessionists. We were utterly unprepared for the descent, and a fight was imminent; but the police explained the matter, and we followed them to the station-house (Independence Hall). We were taken into the Rogues' Gallery, and there deposited our swords and revolvers, and awaited the arrival of Mayor Henry. We showed him our orders from the War Department, which, of course, was sufficient evidence of our character. Our arms were returned, and, on the supposition that the train had left, we went to the Continental to put up for the night at the city's expense. The cause of our arrest was a telegram from the Mayor of Jersey City, stating that forty Southern cadets were on the train, and that their baggage contained small-arms for the South. Under the circumstances the arrest was justifiable. On our arrival in Washington we reported to Colonel Lorenzo Thomas. We have not been assigned to corps yet, but may be tomorrow. I can go into the Engineers by simply saying the word, but I think strongly of the

Third Infantry, which is now on its way here. Tomorrow we commence drilling volunteers, our first duty as officers of the army.

Washington, May 20, 1861.

My dear Sister: I have now really commenced life. No longer a cadet, I am now my own master. How different the circumstances! West Point is in the past. What lies in the future, God only knows! I trust it may be a prosperous and useful career. The time here passes very fast. I worked really hard last week, but do not complain, when I think how much harder the poor privates have to work.

Upton having reported to the Adjutant-General of the Army, was assigned as second-lieutenant to the Fourth Regiment of Artillery, and directed to report to Brigadier-General Mansfield, commanding the troops around Washington. General Mansfield directed him to drill the Twelfth New York Regiment, Colonel Daniel Butterfield commanding, and he was continued on this duty until May 27th, when he was selected as aide-de-camp by Brigadier-General Daniel Tyler, commanding the First Division of the Department of Northeastern Virginia. This officer had graduated from West Point in 1819, and had remained in service until 1834, after which he had been actively employed in constructing and managing railroads in various parts of the United States. But at the first call to arms, and at the sacrifice of his personal interests, he promptly offered his services to the Government, and appeared in Washington at the head of a Connecticut brigade. Although then over sixty-two years of age, he still possessed an active and vigorous mind, a quick and clear perception, and was thoroughly alive to the importance of the vast undertaking of the new Administration. Personally a brave man, and controlled by the most patriotic motives, he was, without doubt, one of the best commanders under whom Upton could at that time have found service. He very readily and properly estimated the undeveloped military qualities of his young aide, and, after a short acquaintance, predicted the greatest success for him in his military career.

The letters which follow exhibit the first impressions of our young soldier upon his entrance into actual service:

Washington, May 24, 1861.

My DEAR Sister: The excitement here continues unabated—in fact, has increased yesterday and today. Last night about eight thousand troops crossed Long Bridge and encamped on the soil of Virginia. This move is the initiative of the war. How soon a pitched battle will be fought I know not, but one must come soon. I am trying my best to be present, but fear I shall be unsuccessful. Today I made application to be assigned to a battery of light artillery, and to-night was told that as soon as an officer was wanted I would be detailed. The Twelfth New York, to which I was assigned, is now on Arlington Heights. I am now on duty with the Second Connecticut, and shall commence drilling them tomorrow.

Washington, June 1, 1861.

Dear Sister: I leave for Virginia to-night at twelve o'clock, aide-de-camp to General Tyler. I will have a horse to ride, and good quarters. My position is admirable. I take your flag with me.

Camp opposite Washington, June 6th.

My dear Sister: I had quite an incident on the night of the march here. We were under orders to march at midnight, to relieve the Twelfth New York at Roach's Mills. I told General Tyler that there were some officers of the Twelfth in Washington, and that they could tell me the route to travel. I mounted my horse and set off for their quarters, with permission to cross the river and reconnoiter the roads leading to the camp of the Twelfth. I got on very well until I reached the center of Long Bridge. There I found that I had the wrong countersign. I showed that I was the bearer of dispatches, and they let me pass on. I had not proceeded far before I was halted by a Jersey sentinel, and, not having the countersign, he would not let me pass. I was referred to the officer of the guard. He sent me to the colonel, but, not satisfying him of my character and mission, he sent me to General [Theodore] Runyon, who forwarded my orders (I was in uniform), but would not release me. He sent his aide to General [Irwin] McDowell, at Arlington, to ascertain my character, and, the general being absent, his adjutant-general, Captain Fry, wrote a note stating that I was all right. I was consequently released, and he gave me the countersign, and instruction to the sergeant of the guard to pass me over the lines. Before passing the lines, I asked the sergeant what the countersign was, so as to be sure. Immediately he halted me and would not let me proceed, until he had sent back to the general to know whether I had it or not. Finally, after a detention of two hours, I was released. While in

43

the general's tent I was guarded by three officers, who took up strategic positions—two slightly in front, the other in rear of me—all armed with revolvers. I had just cleared the lines, when I met General McDowell, who had heard of my arrest in Washington, which had been telegraphed to the War Department, and was on his way to General Runyon to release me. I saw him at Arlington a few days ago, and he told me I would have to pardon the volunteers, for, in their zeal, they often stopped army officers, not excepting himself.

We arrived at Roach's Mills at 5 a. m. Sunday morning. I was then sent out to survey a campground, which took till about noon. I then managed to get about an hour's sleep, the first I had had since the night previous. Yesterday General Tyler sent me out to find the shortest distance from Suter's or Shorter's Hill to Roach's Mills. I started about 9 a. m., and, while the distance is about three miles, after following the various roads to their termini, I finally reached this hill at about one o'clock. I dined with Colonel Farnham, of the Fire Zouaves, and then returned. I found that Major Speidel had posted his sentinels in an open field, and partly in rear of the line of sentinels belonging to a Michigan regiment. I assumed the responsibility of throwing Speidel's sentinels farther to the front, and posted them along a road leading from our camp through a large wood to an open field, thence along a wood-path leading around the field to a small corn-field, where I posted one sentinel, another on the other side of the field, and three more made our line connect with the Michigan line, which extends to Suter's Hill.

After doing this, I reported to the colonel what I had done, and requested Major Speidel to return with me. The major did not like my interference, but he said but little. We took a picket of forty men and set out again. I rode with him up to the first Michigan sentinel, and showed him the route our regiment would have to follow in case we were to re-enforce Suter's Hill, should it be attacked. He immediately fell in with the idea, and called in all his useless sentinels and threw them on the line that I had first designated. I returned then to headquarters and told General Tyler what I had done, accompanying my explanation with a map. When he understood it, he said emphatically two or three times: "That is right; you will do hereafter to go out on your own hook." This was my first compliment from him. I know not why it is, but I stand very well here in the estimation of general officers.

When at Suter's Hill, Lieutenant Snyder [who had been at Fort Sumter] told me that they would like to have me for an aide-de-camp to Colonel Heintzelman. General Tyler last night told me that he should try to keep me as long as he was in service, and that it was very probable that I would be put on McDowell's staff, who commands all the forces on this side.

Fraser's, Va., June 17, 1861.

My dear Sister: We are comfortably settled here, but today or tomorrow we shall move to Roach's Mills. You need not worry about me, for I have all that I want to eat. I mess with the general, and, as he likes good things and has plenty of money, we lack no comforts when they can be obtained. We now have the First and Second Connecticut Volunteers on this side of the river, and the Eighth and Twenty-fifth New York are also brigaded with us.

Virginia does not compare very well with Genesee County. Once in a while we find a good farm, but generally the fences are down and the buildings are old and rickety. Yesterday the general and myself went on the cars with four hundred men of the First Connecticut Volunteers to Vienna, on the Loudon and Hampshire Railroad. Our object was to ascertain whether the road had been disturbed by the rebels. At Vienna the ladies welcomed us by waving handkerchiefs; they were truly glad to see us. The rebels had been there two days before us, and had taken up the lead pipes for bullets. On our return a shot was fired at our men, and took effect in the left shoulder of a soldier standing next to General [Daniel] Tyler. The train was stopped, and the men were thrown into the woods as skirmishers. When I got out of the cars they were firing very rapidly, and I thought then we were going to have a good fight, as we knew there were secesh troops within six miles when we passed up.

Fall's Church, Va., July 1, 1861.

My dear Sister: Is mother as brave as she ought to be? Does she prefer to have me here rather than at home? If she does not, hereafter I will say nothing of projects. Patriotism now should rule affection. I hope she looks at it in this light. We hope to celebrate the 4th of July at Fairfax Court-House. Whether the move will involve a. battle I know not, but I hope it will. Our army has insults to avenge and a flag to defend. Would it not be a glorious celebration of that day to meet and defeat the enemies of our country? Yesterday two companies of the Third Connecticut captured two prisoners and four horses. An ambush was placed within two and a half miles of the chivalrous First South

Carolina. The force was the advanced guard of about thirty or forty of Radford's rangers. A little more coolness and discretion would have enabled them to capture the whole squad. They were very athletic, vigorous men, and one was very courageous and would not give up for some time. They were exceedingly mortified, and I really pitied them. I will fight before I will deliver my sword.

I can remain with General Tyler as long as I please. I know he does not want me to leave, for he has taken the trouble to write to the Assistant Adjutant-General to have me detached, and I think he saw the Secretary of War on the subject. The Fifth United States Artillery is now organizing at Harrisburg, and will not be in the field within two months. Before the expiration of that period there will be hard fighting, and were I to join my company I should lose it all. When it gets into the field I think I shall join it, as I wish to win the reputation of being a good artillery-officer. I have been where I expected a fight, but have not been gratified as yet.

Fall's Church, Va., July 9, 1861.

My dear Sister: Your good letter found me houseless and homeless. General Tyler has turned over the command of the Connecticut brigade to Colonel [Erasmus Darwin] Keyes, and with it our tents, of course. He has not yet located his headquarters, and until then we must trust to our friends for protection. Lieutenant Hascall occupies the same position on Colonel Keyes's staff which I did on General Tyler's, before he was relieved. I meet many of my old West Point instructors daily. Captain Baird (mathematics) is on our staff; Captain Vincent (chemistry) is on General Schenck's staff; Colonel McCook, of tactics, who had my company; Colonel Howard, Captain Williams, and many others. Professor Mahan was out to see us today. He has a very hearty shake of the hand, which I regard as a good index to any man's character. It seems quite strange to associate with these men on terms of equality. I should like to accompany you in your visit at any other time than this; but you know an opportunity will soon present itself for me to be under fire, and I would not miss it for all the world.

During the next nine days, the preliminary movements had all taken place by which McDowell's army had been placed face to face with the enemy.

Our young soldier had been active and zealous in his duty, and had gained the confidence of his general. The latter, in command of the

46

First Division, had, in obedience to the orders of the 16th and 18th of July, moved against Centreville, and had advanced as far as Blackburn's Ford on Bull Run. In the action which this advanced movement had brought about, Upton had aimed the first gun and was in the successful charge made by the First Massachusetts and Second and Third Michigan Regiments against the enemy's position. In this charge he displayed great coolness and dash, and, although he was wounded in the left side and arm by a musket-ball, he did not quit the field, but remained at his post of duty, receiving the commendation of his general for his gallantry. His high anticipations of success against the armed enemies of the country were not realized; and, while the result of the battle of Bull Run dampened his hopes, it did not weaken his faith in the ultimate success of the cause.

The First Battle of Bull Run took place on July 21.—Ed. 2016

His great disappointment at the result of this promising movement is feelingly portrayed in this short but pithy note to his sister:

July 22, 1861.

My dear Sister: I regret to say we are defeated. Our troops fought well, but were badly managed.

The only other letter referring to the battle was written several months after, and refers to a chance meeting with Mr. Lovejoy:

Owen Lovejoy (1811 – 1864) was a lawyer, Congregational minister, abolitionist, and Republican congressman from Illinois.—Ed. 2016

Alexandria, November 25, 1861.

My dear Sister: You spoke of the Hon. Owen Lovejoy. Did I tell you about meeting him at Bull Run? If not, I'll tell you now. General Tyler's division crossed Bull Run about forty rods above Stone Bridge. I crossed with the Sixty-ninth New York, and passed up the opposite bank through a ravine. We had marched but a few rods when we came upon a regiment of secessionists. We were about eight rods from them, and not knowing them to be secessionists we asked them. I was between them and the leading company, and of course rode around the company so that they might open fire. I had but got behind it when my horse was shot and mortally wounded. I dismounted, and remained until the enemy ran, when we ceased firing and resumed the march. I saw my horse a short distance back, and went to him and took off his saddle. I then went forward to a small house where the wounded were being carried. I saw there an old horse, and, as I was an aide-de-camp, I mounted him. I asked for his owner, and Mr. Lovejoy made his appearance. He was assisting in taking care of the wounded, and had exposed his life freely. I told him I was an aide and my horse had been shot, and asked for his. He gave him to me immediately, and I consigned to his care a valuable field-glass. I rejoined the staff, and changed the horse with an orderly. On the retreat my arm pained me, and I procured a steady horse belonging to the quartermaster's department. Mr. Lovejoy's horse was ridden by a member of our staff, and was returned to him in Washington. I have a high respect for Mr. Lovejoy, because he fights for his principles and is a brave man.

Upon recovering from his wound, Upton, having been assigned to the artillery, was ordered, August 14, 1861, to duty in Battery D, Second United States Artillery, which was located in the defenses of Washington, south of the Potomac. During the interval of rest and reorganization of the Army of the Potomac, he remained at Alexandria with his battery, which was commanded by Captain Richard Arnold until the latter part of October, then by Captain Platt, and, before leaving again for active service, by Upton himself. In the daily routine of camp-life there was much to be done to make the battery efficient for field-service, and that this was thoroughly well done, both by officers and men, was shown in its subsequent record. The few incidents well to note before the beginning of the Peninsular campaign, as well as the impressions that occupied his mind, are given in the following letters:

Arnold's Battery, Alexandria, August 31, 1861.

My dear Sister: Since I last wrote you we have again changed camp. Captain Arnold sent me forward to locate our ground, and has honored me by naming the camp after me. We are on high ground, and not so far from the enemy as before. Our brigade is now commanded by General Mitchell* (the renowned astronomer). I hope he may be as proficient in the science of war as in astronomy. Everything is quiet in front; occasionally there is picket-firing. Yesterday I visited our pickets at Bailey's Cross-roads, and saw again the secession flag, and heard the discharge of musketry. Our pickets were then having a brush with theirs. One of their officers was shot. His rank is not known, but he was probably a valuable officer, for the flag was lowered to half-mast, and remained so during the da-. They have a field-work one and a quarter miles from Bailey's, on Munson's Hill, I have been on the hill, but it was when at Fall's Church. They could easily be dislodged by planting two batteries—one at Bailey's, the other near Willie Throckmorton's house—and attacking them with infantry between the batteries.... I paid a visit to the officers of the Second Maine, and they gave me a hearty welcome. You will remember that we charged up the hill together. I saw the color-bearer who behaved so nobly, carrying forward our flag, planting it until the men came up, and then carrying it forward again. If I ever attain a position to reward anybody, he shall be remembered.

*Ormsby MacKnight Mitchel (1810 – October 30, 1862)—Ed. 2016

Alexandria, September 30, 1861.

My dear Sister: Yesterday we had a regular field-day. We marched at 5 a. m. for Bailey's Cross-roads, and on arriving there found Munson's Hill in possession of our troops. We then marched for Mason's Hill, where the rebels also had fortifications, but they had deserted them. My section was brought into battery commanding the Fairfax road, but as only a few cavalry showed themselves at times we did not fire. We returned to Bailey's at 3 p. m., and encamped, expecting to remain there all night, but at supper orders were received to return to our old camp. In twenty minutes we were ready to move, and at half-past seven were at our old home. The works at Munson's and Mason's Hills were mere scarecrows—nothing but shells which I could and did ride my horse right over. At Munson's they had a wooden Columbiad pointed over the parapet, which gave rise to the report that they had heavy guns.

The conduct of our troops was disgraceful beyond expression. They burned buildings, destroyed furniture, stole dishes, chairs, etc., killed chickens, pigs, calves, and everything they could eat. They would take nice sofa-chairs, which they had not the slightest use for, and ten minutes after throw them away. Talk about the barbarity of the rebels! I believe them to be Christians compared to our thieves. The houses entered yesterday belonged mostly to Union people, yet they were unmolested by the rebels. One of our volunteer majors, walked up to a looking-glass, worth about twenty dollars, and deliberately put his foot through it. I wish I had witnessed it. He would have had the benefit of a court-martial.

Alexandria, October 4, 1861.

My dear Sister: I want you to cease worrying about me. It does no good either to yourself or me, and it gives me no comfort whatever. You have the New York papers daily, and undoubtedly, were accident to befall me, you would hear of it through them first. If I am to be killed in battle, no earthly power can avert it. My fate I know not. Whatever it may be I am ready and willing to meet it. I am fighting for right, and trust in God to defend me. If it be his will I desire no more happy or glorious death than on the battlefield in the defense of our flag. I owe all to the Government, and, in return, the Government shall have all. Perhaps I shall have a great mission to perform; if so, I shall not fail to ask wisdom from "Him who giveth liberally and upbraideth not." You spoke of mother's prayers—they are offered in faith. I wish I had her steadfastness.

It is now quite probable that we shall remain here for some time. I hope not, but if not ready it is expedient to remain on the defensive. The great points of interest are now Missouri and Kentucky. Two big battles may be expected very soon, one in each State; but the grand one will take place when the Army of the Potomac takes the offensive.

Alexandria, November 13, 1861.

Dear SISTER: My views are not changed; I am opposed to Southern slavery in every form, viewed in any light—political, social, or moral. I have taken an oath "to bear true allegiance to the United States," and I hope to observe that oath. Slavery is the cause of the rebellion, and I believe it is God's providence that it shall be overthrown. It will be the consequence, not the effect, of the war. After the war is ended there will be a great influx of Northern men into the Southern States; their views will gradually triumph and slavery must yield. The rebels wish to establish a monarchy, and are fighting for that object. We are fighting for the Government, and against that object.

Alexandria, November 23, 1861.

My dear Sister: Time passes so rapidly now that it is hard to take cognizance of it. This is a cold, bleak night, and the poor soldiers at the outposts must suffer from cold; our men even suffer in their tents. I can hardly look forward to winter without a shudder—not that I have any anxiety for myself, but for the private soldier, whose covering for the night is but one thin blanket.

Alexandria, March 26, 1862.

My dear Sister: We are still at Alexandria, expecting to embark, but not knowing exactly when, possibly on Sunday. We bide our time patiently, knowing that hard fighting awaits us. We are promised the first blow, and hope to give it soon. Yesterday the ladies at Commodore Wilkes's presented the company with an elegant American flag for a guidon. I told them I would never return unless the flag did, and the promise shall be kept.

General McDowell reviewed his corps yesterday. It is forty thousand strong, and has sixty-eight pieces of artillery. As he was riding along he asked, "Which is Upton's battery?" which shows I am known to him. Give me one chance, and I shall be quite contented; and, if I don't acquit myself with honor, you will never see me again.

It does not fall within the scope of this memoir to analyze or to discuss the great campaigns of the war, and it is sufficient for our purpose, in describing the fortunes of a junior officer, to give a mere outline of the important movements, dwelling alone on those events which had their influence in his military development, and in which he was an actor.

The Army of the Potomac after the battle of Bull Run was without organization and discipline. Although its elements were as good as this country could then furnish, it could not be made an efficient instrument for the defense of the country, or the suppression of the rebellion, without organization and enforced discipline. Neither men nor officers knew how to take care of their own health, how to cook their rations, or to shelter themselves from inclement weather. These things are learned only by bitter experience. The reports of the regimental and other commanders of the Army of the Potomac, of the chief medical officer, the quartermaster-general, the commissary-general, and other staff-officers, if attentively read, will be found full of instruction on these points. They clearly show that an army is something more than a body of armed and uniformed citizens gathered in haste from their civil pursuits.

From the time when McClellan* took command of the Army of the Potomac until it moved to the Peninsula the improvement in its efficiency was marked and permanent. Without this improvement it never could have so well performed its allotted task, nor become the great dependence upon which the Government could with security rely.

*George Brinton McClellan (1826–1885) was a controversial figure in the war. Considered brilliant by many military men, he was loved by the soldiers of the Army of the Potomac. He was the one most responsible for organizing and training that army. But he clashed repeatedly with President Lincoln (for whom he had little respect) and Secretary of War, Edwin Stanton. McClellan was twice placed in command and twice removed. While still listed as an active soldier but not serving, he ran as the Democratic candidate for president against Lincoln in 1864. McClellan believed the Union should be restored but was not an advocate of emancipation. He was later governor of New Jersey.—Ed. 2016

McDowell's corps, originally intended to form part of the army by which McClellan was to advance on Richmond by way of the James River Peninsula, was, at the last moment, retained as a cover to Washington. Upton's battery belonged to Franklin's division of this corps, and it was not until April 22d that this division reported to McClellan at Yorktown. On May 7th it effected a landing at West Point, Va., overcoming at that place a spirited resistance on the part of the enemy. In this engagement Upton handled his battery with coolness, and it was commended for its excellent firing by General Franklin in his report. Upton was now where he had all along desired to be—in actual service, in the command of a battery of artillery. The reputation of a battery is that of its captain. The latter must be cool yet resolute, quick of eye, decided in character, incapable of demoralization, and daring enough to gather all the fruits which his position and opportunities offer. These traits Upton possessed thoroughly. He had that *coup d'oeil militaire* which enabled him at a glance to gather in all the peculiarities of the military position, and which were at once indelibly printed in his mind, ready for utilization at the critical moment. The uproar of battle steadied him and gave him the full and active possession of his faculties. It is to these qualities we must attribute the high praise which his conduct evoked on the part of every commander with whom he served.

From West Point he moved with Franklin's division to the Chickahominy; and at the battle of Gaines Mills, June 27th, we find his battery assigned to the brigade of General John Newton, and with it participating in the action, doing excellent service in this stubborn contest.

During the seven days' battle [June 25 to July 1, 1862] on the retreat to the James River, Upton's battery performed a distinguished part, especially at the battle of Glendale or Charles City Cross-roads. In this action Upton was in Slocum's division of the Sixth Corps, who says in his report of the battle that "the artillery commanded by Upton and Porter was exceedingly well served," and that "the position was mainly defended by the artillery, which on this, as on all other occasions, was most admirably served. Of Upton's battery (D), Second Artillery, and Porter's battery (A), First Massachusetts Artillery, I cannot speak too highly. The officers and men of both these batteries have on all occasions manifested that coolness and bravery so necessary to this branch of the service."

We next hear of Upton through the official reports at Crampton's Gap, Md. In the meantime McClellan's army had been withdrawn from the James; Pope had fought unsuccessfully the second battle of Bull Run; and McClellan had again been put in command of the Army of the Potomac, and was following after Lee, to cut him off or bring him to battle, during his invasion of Maryland. The affair at Crampton's Gap, September 14, 1862, was one of the minor actions preliminary to Antietam,* September 17, 1862. Upton was at that time in command of the Artillery Brigade of four batteries, twenty-six guns, of the First Division of the Sixth Army Corps. He had obtained this position as a just reward for his success in the previous campaign, and the promotion being within the province of his immediate commanders to bestow, was a marked evidence of his own merit. His letters and the extracts from official reports show clearly the part he had taken in the Antietam campaign.

Antietam remains today the bloodiest single day of fighting in U.S. history.—Ed. 2016

Camp near Bakersville, Md., September 27, 1862.

My dear Sister: The pleasant campaign of Maryland has closed with the expulsion of the rebel invaders. From the time we left Alexandria (the second day after my return) till the close of the battle of Antietam, I never spent any hours more agreeably or enjoyed myself better. We lived well, marched through a lovely country, had beautiful weather, magnificent scenery, and above all two glorious battles. At the battle of Crampton's Gap, although not actively engaged, I was under fire. It was, however, at the battle of Antietam that I had full swing. The artillery is a pretty arm, and makes a great deal of noise. From 2 p. m. till dark we fed the rebels on shells, spherical case, and solid shot. They did not appreciate our kindness, and entertained us in like manner. Shells and case-shot I don't care anything about, but round shot are great demoralizers. The sharp-shooters were very busy all the time, and annoyed us very much. I took my field-glass and stepped behind a gate-post to rest it, so that I could get a steady view. The instant I got behind it, the post was struck by a Minie-ball. It is no exaggeration to say that I was fired at a dozen times during the day. The infantry fighting was terrible. I do not believe there has been harder fighting this century than that between Hooker and the rebels in the morning. I have heard of the "dead lying in heaps," but never saw it till at this battle. Whole ranks fell together.

The trials of some of the wounded were horrible. I did not know it at the time, but, during all our firing, a wounded rebel lay under a fence about forty feet in front of the muzzles of our guns. Between their roar and the bursting shells from his own friends, the poor fellow must have suffered beyond conception. One of our captains lay wounded in a brick school-house, through which several of our shells and solid shot passed, hurling the bricks in every direction, but, strange to say, not injuring him. He died of his wound the next day. His dying message was to tell his friends that "he had been in nine battles, and that he died a brave man." A good soldier.

In regard to the part played by Upton at Antietam, Colonel Irving, one of the brigade commanders of the Second Division of the Sixth Corps, reports:

"About half-past four o'clock, Captain Upton, Chief of Artillery of Slocum's division, rode to my line, and, after we had examined the ground in front of the left attentively, I decided to accept the battery which he earnestly advised me to have placed there. Not a minute could be lost; the enemy were massing in front with the evident design of throwing a powerful column against my left, and they could not be seen except from that part of the line. I instantly sent word to Major-General [William Farrar] Baldy Smith, who approved the movement, and I requested Captain Upton to order up the battery, which came into action very promptly and opened with three rifled guns, which, after playing on the masses of the enemy with great effect for half an hour, were withdrawn, and their places supplied by a battery of Napoleon guns, the fire of which was very destructive; these guns were of inestimable value to us, and the coolness and the precision with which they were served deserve the highest commendation, and it gives me great pleasure to acknowledge how much I was indebted to Captain Upton, and to the officers and men under his command."

REGIMENTAL AND BRIGADE COMMANDER

Upton's peculiar fitness for the profession of arms was evident to all who came in contact with him, and the impression made by his intrepidity in battle was not easy to forget. The attention of the authorities of the State of New York was early directed toward those officers of the regular army who were fit to command its regiments, and likely to reflect honor upon the State; and the choice fell upon Upton for the command of the One Hundred and Twenty-first Regiment, New York Volunteers. This regiment had been raised in Herkimer and Otsego Counties, in obedience to the call of the President in August, 1862, for three hundred thousand volunteers. By August 30th the regiment was ready to leave for the front, under the command of Colonel Richard Franchot. On the 3d of September it reached Washington; on the 14th and 17th it participated in the battles of Crampton's Gap and Antietam, and on the 23d of October it received its new colonel, Emory Upton, who had been so commissioned by Governor Fenton on the 9th of October. One of the first to congratulate the young colonel and to commend the regiment to his best devotion was its first commander, Colonel Franchot, who, having been elected to Congress, relinquished the command to take his seat as a Representative. Upton had, however, been ordered, August 14th, to duty at the Military Academy, which order was, to his great gratification, revoked to enable him to take command of his regiment. From this time, therefore, his connection with the regular army was merely that of his regimental rank as an artillery-officer, and his subsequent career was identified with the volunteers.

The rank and file of his regiment were made up of the best men the country then produced—men of brawn and muscle, urged by the highest patriotism to enlist for a service that promised hard fighting and the severest trials. They deserve the highest commendation, and they made for themselves a glorious record. Engaged in every battle fought by the Army of the Potomac from Antietam to the close of the war, their devotion was attested by their constantly thinned ranks and the honorable scars of the survivors. They were readily amenable to the strict discipline needed for success, and heartily

56

gave unquestioned obedience to the gallant soldier who was their animating spirit and led their advance in the assault.

On the occasion of the reunion of the survivors of the regiment in 1878, Major Douglas Campbell gave fitting testimony as to the causes which contributed to the gratifying record attained by the regiment while under the command of Colonel Upton. He says:

"This record was not the result of chance; it was due mainly to two causes: The first was the material of which the regiment was composed; men who went out to fight for principle must make good soldiers. The second was the influence of the man that we were fortunate enough to secure as our leader. Earnestness is the chief secret of success in life; of all the men that I have ever met, no one was more thoroughly in earnest than Colonel Upton. Bred at West Point, he was but twenty-two years of age when he donned the eagles and the badge of the One Hundred and Twenty-first. The first day he made to the officers a little speech about what he expected of the regiment. I went away feeling that we had indeed found a man. How the regiment was affected is shown by its subsequent record. At first some of the boys thought he was severe in discipline and drill; but when people began flocking from distant encampments to witness our dress parades, and when in battle they saw the regiment standing like a solid wall, these very men thanked the colonel. In discipline he was stern, but it was only the sternness of a soldier; below it was as warm a heart as ever beat. When we lay for that fearful night at Belle Plain Landing, without tents, fire, or food, in sleet and mud, which froze before morning to a solid mass, the field-officers alone had a tent. Upton gave up his couch to a sick lieutenant, and, rolled in a blanket, lay upon the ground. A day or so afterward I heard a conversation between the officers who occupied the tent. The others, it seems, rested comfortably, but Upton said he could not sleep, thinking of the poor fellows outside who had no shelter. You remember that when he joined us we had a very large sick list. Upton came to us from a battery of regular artillery, and for some days was absent a large portion of the time. We supposed he was visiting his old associates. A few weeks afterward I met a friend who belonged to a regular regiment. He said to me: 'What is the colonel of your regiment doing? Is he studying medicine?' I asked what he meant, and he replied, 'Why, for a long time he came over here almost every day, and passed his whole time in our hospitals, talking to our surgeons, and studying our medical system.' That explained why the health of the regiment improved so rapidly after he took command. In those early days I remember seeing a sentinel, who for some fault had been sent for to his tent, coming out crying as if his heart would break. When he could speak, I asked him what was the matter, and through his tears he answered: 'The colonel has been talking to me about allowing my gun to be taken away on post. He spoke of the danger which might come to the army from neglect of duty like that, and spoke in such a way that I felt as if I were unworthy to be a soldier. He said he would not punish me, but I would rather spend a month in the guard-house than have him look and talk so.' That soldier never failed in his duty afterward. Such was our colonel in camp—watchful of his men, studious of their health and comfort, kind-hearted as a woman; but in battle he was terrible. You all know that, however, as well as or better than I do. The regiment went everywhere, but he was always in advance. Were he here, I should have said nothing of all this, for he is as modest as he is brave; but, as he is absent, I could not refrain from rendering to his services my little tribute of praise. Certainly in this, the first address at our reunion, it is not out of place to express our gratitude to the man who helped so largely to make this regiment what it was."

The testimony given by Major Campbell is in keeping with Upton's well-known traits of character. He was ever alive to the wants and necessities of his men. He jealously guarded their interests, and never for a moment lost sight of anything that would conduce to their health and comfort; but he likewise exacted of them that prompt and unhesitating obedience without which proper discipline cannot be maintained. The following letter shows how well Major Campbell had estimated the character of his new colonel:

Belle Plain, Va., December 7, 1862.

My dear Sister: We marched from Stafford Court-House to White Oak Church three days ago. Day before yesterday our brigade marched

58

to this point, the confluence of the Potomac River and Potomac Creek. When we arrived it was snowing and quite cold, and we had to encamp on the plain. There were no woods to break the wind, no wood to build fires, and the men were wet to the skin; the ground was covered with snow and water, and with but a thin shelter-tent over their heads, and nothing but the cold ground to lie on and one blanket for a covering, you can imagine how the poor soldiers fared that night. Yesterday it was clear and cold, and last night colder than any night last winter. The ice froze thick enough to bear a horse. Today I took the regiment from the plain to the woods—dense cedar and a high ridge—to protect them from the wind, and to-night they are very comfortable, although it is still very cold. I like the regiment very much. The men know that they will be taken care of, and they are quite contented.

His new regiment formed a part of the brigade in which he had won distinction, and this more prominent command called out all the energy of his mind and body. In the battle of Fredericksburg, December 13, 1862, he had an opportunity of testing the soldierly qualities of his men. Here his gallant bearing and coolness under fire were so striking that he won the affection of his men, and they behaved so like veterans that mutual confidence was from that time well established.

The first time that his regiment engaged the enemy seriously was in the battle of Salem Heights, May 3, 1863. His official report to the brigade commander says:

"The regiment was deployed to the left of the plank road, about three miles from Fredericksburg, and had advanced in line of battle nearly a mile when it came upon our skirmishers in the edge of a belt of timber, about three hundred yards through, beyond which was Salem Chapel. The skirmishers reported the enemy in line of battle in the opposite edge of the woods.

"About 5.30 p. m. I received an order to push rapidly through the woods and engage the enemy, who were supposed to be hastily withdrawing. I sent the report of the enemy's position to the general commanding the brigade, and immediately advanced the line. The regiment advanced steadily to within fifty yards of the opening, when it was assailed by a heavy fire of musketry from the enemy concealed behind a ditch. The fire was received without creating the slightest confusion. The regiment moved forward with a cheer about twenty yards farther. The enemy opposite the center and left wing broke, but rallied again about twenty or thirty yards to his rear. The Ninety-sixth Pennsylvania now came up to our left and the Twenty-third New Jersey to our right, but opened fire before coming on our line. Lieutenant-Colonel Olcott endeavored to have the Twenty-third New Jersey charge, but without success. The firing became very heavy on both sides, and was maintained about five minutes. It was impossible to remain longer.

"Having lost nearly two hundred in killed and wounded, the regiment fell back to a crest four hundred and fifty yards this side of the woods, where the colors were planted.... It was the first time the regiment had ever been in action. It went into the engagement with four hundred and fifty-three, and suffered a loss of forty-four killed, one hundred and fifteen wounded, and one hundred and ten missing, making a total of two hundred and sixty-nine. Notwithstanding the severe loss inflicted, it came out of the action without any demoralization, and is again ready for any service that may be imposed upon it."

General Bartlett says:

"Colonel E. Upton, commanding the One Hundred and Twenty-first New York, in the battle of Salem Heights, led his regiment into action in a masterly and fearless manner, and maintained the unequal contest to the last with unflinching nerve and marked ability, and the men of his regiment, in this, their first battle, won for themselves the proud title of soldiers."

Shortly after the battle of Chancellorsville [April 30 to May 6, 1863], Lee undertook the second invasion of Maryland, and pushed forward into Pennsylvania. The command of the Army of the Potomac had fallen to General [George Gordon] Meade, and the sequence of events brought the opposing forces into conflict in the decisive battle of Gettysburg. Colonel Upton's regiment, forming a part of the Sixth Corps, reached the battlefield on the afternoon of the 2d of July, after a forced march, but yet in time to render important service to the hard-pressed Union left flank.

The following letter shows how fully he appreciated the importance of the events in which he participated:

Gettysburg, Pa., July 4, 1863.

My dear Sister: Yesterday was a glorious day for the country and the Army of the Potomac. Lee attacked our army in position about 2 p. M-, and was completely repulsed, with a loss of three brigadier-generals, thirty stands of colors, three thousand 4 prisoners, and a heavy loss in killed and wounded. The blow fell on the Second Corps, which has greatly distinguished itself. The battle began on the 1st; Major-General [John] Reynolds was killed that day, and his corps badly cut up. On the 2d, Lee attacked, and was repulsed all around. The Sixth Corps, on the night of the 1st, lay at Manchester. It commenced its march for Gettysburg about 10 p. m., and arrived here about 4 p. m. on the 2d, a distance of thirty-two miles. We arrived just in time to re-enforce our left, which was hard pressed by Longstreet, and slowly giving way. Ten minutes later, and the battle had been lost.

Lee's attack yesterday [Pickett's Charge] was imposing and sublime. For about ten minutes I watched the contest, when it seemed that the weight of a hair would have turned the scales. Our men fought most gallantly. The rebels began to give way, and soon retreated in utter confusion. Shortly after, the enemy on our left also retreated. I think Lee will evacuate Maryland and Pennsylvania at once. He sought this battle, and was badly whipped. If we are reinforced, he will suffer terribly before recrossing the Potomac. Generals [Winfield Scott] Hancock and [John] Gibbon were wounded yesterday. Generals Paul and Weed were killed on the 2d. Our entire loss is about twelve thousand killed and wounded; the rebel loss in killed, wounded, and prisoners, will be between fifteen and twenty thousand. Kilpatrick lost some prisoners yesterday, but he won a splendid reputation. General [Francis] Bartlett has taken command of Newton's old division, and today I was assigned to the command of his brigade by order of General Wright. The command of a brigade is a half-way step between colonel and brigadier-general, and I shall try to take the full step in the next battle. Our division has been considerably under fire during the battle, but was not actively engaged. Some were struck, but none killed.

General Paul was not killed but severely wounded so as to expect that he could not live. For an excellent civilian account of the three days of battle, including time spent with the dying General Weed, see

61

If possible, we ought to fight Lee not far from Hagerstown, and also immediately after he crosses the Potomac. By judicious management, he must go back to Virginia. Yesterday's contest seems the decisive battle of the war. Our men are in good spirits over the success. The Sixth Corps marched from Fairfax Court-House to this place in six days, a distance of one hundred and nine miles, eighteen miles per day.

How is brother Henry's shoulder? Have him keep perfectly quiet, and not think of returning until able to do duty.

After the decisive struggle at Gettysburg, the enemy succeeded in recrossing the Potomac, and in taking up again a defensive position. They were closely pressed by the Union troops in their retreat, and, for a while, both armies waited each other's movements without showing any disposition to take the initiative. Upton's letters give clearly the sequence of events in which he was engaged, and the active thoughts which occupied his mind are happily expressed in terse and vigorous language. It is to be remembered that the criticisms in which he indulges in the private letters to his home are not the results of subsequent digested study when the whole field was clearly presented to his view, but the rapid conclusions which his active and brilliant military mind abstracted from passing occurrences based on the fragmentary knowledge he possessed of what was going on throughout the theatre of war.

New Baltimore, Va, August 6, 1863.

My dear Sister: I have seldom seen, even in Virginia, so hot a day as this. The heat penetrates everywhere, and in the shade one tosses about in vain to seek comfort. Once in a while a cool current of air passes over us, but very rarely. It was the same kind of weather we had at Harrison's Landing, only in a greater degree. Our locality is much healthier, on account of its elevation. We are about twenty miles from the Blue Ridge, and exactly at the southern terminus of Bull Run, or Pignut Mountains. The rest of the division is at Warrenton. My brigade and a battery of artillery hold this point, and you see, therefore, that it is quite a responsible command. Mosby, with his guerrillas, infests this locality, and if he becomes impertinent he may get chastised, but I do not think there will be much trouble. Both armies seem to have taken a defensive position, and are gathering themselves for the storm that will burst upon them probably in November. I think it decidedly good policy on our part to wait. Our armies at all points should be re-enforced so as to far outnumber the enemy. In the next struggle there ought not to be the possibility of defeat. We have got men enough, and we have only to bring them out. In future, the hardest fighting will be in the East. This is necessarily so, from the fact that in the West our lines of communication are so long that the various armies have to pay the utmost attention to guarding them. Grant can scarcely move from Vicksburg; his first objective would be Meridian, one hundred and fifty miles. The enemy might not fight there, but fall back behind the Tombigbee, and dispute its passage. If Grant goes to Mobile, his operations would have to cease with its capture, for the next point to be taken would be Montgomery, as far distant as Meridian. This could be accomplished with adequate force, but can't we better employ what we have? I'll answer that, after looking to [General William] Rosecrans. Rosecrans has from the first been paralyzed by his long line of communications. I do not see how he can advance, except by accumulating supplies sufficient to last six months, independent of communications. These would have to be collected at Tullahoma, which would have to be intrenched and guarded by a large and brave garrison. Nashville would be too far in his rear for this depot. These supplies accumulated at Tullahoma would form a new base of operations. His army could push on to Chattanooga, and, sooner or later, to Atlanta, surely as far as Dalton. I do not think it would pay to move even farther south than Dalton, Georgia.

The Army of the Potomac is in Virginia. You now have the present position of affairs. Now where shall we strike? Grant has about ninety thousand men, [General Nathaniel] Banks say forty thousand. Detach twenty-five thousand from Grant to Banks. The latter, with the gunboats, should be able to keep the Mississippi River clear. Now assemble all the water transportation (impress it, of course) the Government can find at Vicksburg, sufficient for the remaining sixty-five thousand of Grant's force. The enemy will expect, of course, that he will attack Mobile. Let him effect a landing thereabout; let the gunboats attack the forts at the entrance of the harbor, but let his main fleet continue on its course to Port Royal, South Carolina, and then let him come down upon the rear of Charleston. His feint at Mobile, if well-played, would deceive the enemy so long that he could not transfer his troops by rail in time to avert the disaster at Charleston. You may not see what is to be gained by possessing Charleston. In the first place, it is their principal harbor for blockade-runners. Secessionists admit that prices of all foreign articles would be doubled. The moral effect would be great on both sides, but all this would be insignificant compared with its strategical importance. Once ours, the army would move rapidly upon Augusta, which, if accomplished, would, like Vicksburg, again divide the Confederacy. Lee's army would be completely isolated from Bragg and Johnston. The conclusion of the rebellion would speedily follow. The rebels are in a bad plight. In their place, I think I would now re-enforce Lee to such an extent from Bragg and Johnston that he could take the offensive against this army and drive it back to Washington. They could then be again returned south, and might arrive in time to save Charleston, should it be our plan to attack it. They can safely withdraw troops from the West, just on account of the difficulty we experience in feeding our armies. That the rebellion will be crushed does not admit of a doubt. The action of the Government in reference to drafting is manly, and inspires us with confidence in its ultimate success. I have branched off a little in this letter because you have often requested it. I do not expect that the plan proposed will be adopted, but it will do no harm to speculate—perhaps I may be right; if so, of course it would strengthen my confidence in my judgment.

The surrender of Vicksburg to Grant came just one day after Meade's great victory at Gettysburg, July 4.—Ed. 2016

Warrenton, Va., November 6, 1863.

Dear Brother: We are again around this "secesh" town, which we left about September 12th. We then marched to the Rapidan. The rebel fortifications appearing too formidable, Meade did not attack. Lee then began a series of manoeuvres which (I can, but ought not to criticise) threw us back behind Bull Run. Lee fell back immediately without trying to force battle. We followed up leisurely to this point, where we arrived October 20th.

I sometimes get discouraged because of our not accomplishing decided results, but patience is a military as well as a social virtue, and therefore I continue to hope. I am reading *Plutarch's Lives*, and I cannot fail to see the charm success lends to military life. Victorious in every battle, courage rewarded in every struggle, who could not follow a Caesar or a Napoleon? Success begets confidence and resolution, which is a battle half won. No soldier in the world can equal the American, if properly commanded. He possesses all the enthusiasm of the French, and the bull-dog' tenacity which has always characterized the English. He only wants a general who can call out his good qualities, or one who comprehends his nature. I think our generals betray in some instances total ignorance of human nature. They fail to appeal to the emotions or passions of their men. You know not the good a single word does a soldier when he is under fire. He feels that his commanding officer is directing him and looking at his actions. I have never heard our generals utter a word of encouragement, either before or after entering a battle. I have never seen them ride along the lines and tell each regiment that it held an important position, and that it was expected to hold it to the last. I have never heard them appeal to the love every soldier has for his colors or to his patriotism. Neither have I ever seen a general thank his troops after the action for the gallantry they have displayed.

My brief experience has taught me the value of a few words. At Blackburn's Ford, July 18, 1861, I appealed to the patriotism of the Twelfth New York. The way they fought after it assured me that they appreciated the remarks. But the most striking instance occurred at Gettysburg. We came on to the field about 4 P. m., and were held in reserve until about 6 p. m. We were then moved up to the left to support the Third and Fifth Corps, which had been repulsed. The men were tired, weary, and foot-sore. They had marched, since 10 p. m. the preceding night, thirty-two miles. Stray bullets were passing over our heads when I turned to address them. You know I am but poorly gifted with speech, but I felt the fate of the nation depended upon the issue of that battle. A feeling of enthusiasm possessed me so electrifying that, for the first time in my life, words and actions came to me spontaneously. In a few words, I told them how momentous was the issue, how much the country expected of us. I appealed to their pride and patriotism; I promised to lead, and asked them to follow. Their eyes kindled, order replaced despondency, and the noble fellows burst out into a cheer that would have raised the hair of a confronting rebel. From that instant I had as much confidence in them as in myself. How well they fought is attested by the battle of Salem Chapel. Of four hundred and fifty-three taken into action, two hundred and twenty-seven were killed and wounded, and this in their first fight. The killed amounted to eighty. Of these, sixty-two were left dead on the field; seventeen were from one company. How short the range, is shown by the ratio of killed to wounded (eighty to one hundred and forty-seven, or less than one to two), whereas the usual ratio is one to four or five. Nearly the whole loss was inflicted at a range varying between four and eight rods, and in the space of about five minutes. The conduct of the regiment challenged the admiration of the enemy, but it was not mentioned by our commanders, where others with a loss little more than half as large were mentioned in the highest terms.

I had expected brother Henry to return today, but he has not yet arrived. He had a most severe wound, and has borne it like a hero. His courage in battle is of the highest order.

Upton, although now in command of a brigade, had not yet attained the actual rank of a brigadier-general. He could not be blind to his own fitness for the desired promotion, and, although he shows in his letters of this period a restiveness because of the delay in the only recognition which the Government could bestow, he never failed to do his whole duty in whatever service he was called upon to perform. In the assault of the rebel intrenchments, or *tete de pont*, at Rappahannock Station, he led his Second Brigade of the First Division of the Sixth Corps again to victory. In this action, his clear perception, ready courage, the rare skill with which he led his brigade, gained for it a brilliant victory over a much superior enemy, both in numbers and strength of position. His own story, told with the modesty of a hero, and with a due appreciation of the great soldierly qualities of his immediate commander, General David A. Russell, is thus graphically related:

Headquarters Second Brigade, November 15, 1863.

My dear Sister: Doubtless you have seen through the papers that this brigade has been engaged with the enemy, and that it met with astonishing success. There are many accounts of the battle extant, but I will give you the true version, believing it will interest you all. Our division left Warrenton at daylight on the 7th. General Bartlett being ordered to the Fifth Corps, I fell in command of the brigade. We marched to the railroad near Rappahannock Station, halted there till dusk, when the fight began. From one o'clock till sunset there was considerable artillery-firing and skirmishing, but no serious loss was inflicted on either side. At dusk, General Russell, who commanded the division, conceived the idea of capturing the enemy's works by a *coup-de-main*. To this end he brought forward one regiment apparently to relieve the skirmishers, who had been in the front all day, and another to act as a support. The enemy saw the whole operation, but supposing it simply a relief, paid but little attention to the matter. The first or old line of skirmishers were notified of the intention, the second line came up to where the first lay, when both rushed upon the enemy's redoubts, and were almost inside before the enemy recovered from his astonishment. This gallant attack was made by the Sixth Maine, which suffered very heavily, the Fifth Wisconsin, and two companies of the One Hundred and Twenty-first New York. Four guns, one color, and two hundred prisoners were captured upon the spot. The bridge, by which the enemy maintained communication with the south bank of the river, was now commanded by our men, who held the redoubts. Seeing his retreat thus intercepted, the enemy made desperate efforts to recapture the works, and had well-nigh succeeded, when General Russell sent me an order to bring forward two of my regiments to his assistance. The One Hundred and Twenty-first New York and Fifth Maine were in the first line; I immediately ordered them forward, and, to avoid any delay, directed them to load while marching; this done, telling them we were wanted to help hold the works captured, they took the double-quick and soon arrived to the support of our hard-pressed comrades. Upon arriving, General Russell pointed out a rifle-pit from which the enemy maintained an enfilading fire, and he ordered me to charge the rifle-pit and hold it. The work was on the summit of a gently rising knoll. Their banners could be plainly seen outstanding against the sky, while their saucy heads appearing everywhere above the parapets forewarned us how deadly might be our task. My orders were distinct: it remained to execute them in the safest, surest, and most satisfactory manner. Under cover of darkness we formed within a hundred yards of their works. I told the Fifth Maine that the troops from Maine had won laurels on every field, and that the gallant Fifth must not be behind them. A few words to the One Hundred and Twenty-first New York sufficed to rouse their determination to the highest pitch. I directed them to unsling knapsacks and fix bayonets. Then giving the strictest orders not to fire, we advanced at quick time to within thirty yards of the rifle-pit, when the order to charge was given. The work was carried at the point of the bayonet. The enemy fought stubbornly over their colors, but were overpowered. To execute my orders we had only to remain where we were, but a more brilliant success was in store. The celebrated Louisiana brigade of Stonewall Jackson's old division lay behind the rifle-pits to our right. On their banners were inscribed "Cedar Run,"

67

"Manassas second," "Winchester," "Harper's Ferry," "Sharpsburg," "Fredericksburg," "Chancellorsville," and "Gettysburg." Word was brought me that the enemy on our right was in confusion; he could also be seen apparently moving to his rear. Without waiting for further orders, I sent Captain Hall of the staff to report to General Russell that we had performed the task assigned to us and made immediate dispositions to attack. Major Mather, of the One Hundred and Twenty-first New York, with a portion of his regiment, was ordered to seize the bridge and to arrest those who might attempt to swim the river. Colonel Edwards, of the Fifth Maine, with a part of his own and the One Hundred and Twenty-first Regiments, was ordered to charge at double-quick and not to fire. The remainder of the two regiments was held in reserve, should the enemy offer resistance. I told our men not to fire, and stated in a loud tone that four lines of battle were supporting us. The enemy being deceived, supposed a vastly superior force was advancing, and the entire brigade of the enemy laid down their arms. The colonel commanding surrendered personally to me. These movements resulted in capturing seven colors, one hundred and three commissioned officers, thirteen hundred and thirty-seven enlisted men, and twelve hundred and twenty-five stand of arms. It was all done after dark, when one could not distinguish friend from foe, and with a force numbering five hundred and sixty-eight, officers and men included. Our total loss in the two regiments amounted to sixty-three killed and wounded. I think the slight loss, in a great degree, may be attributed to our not firing. The enemy hearing the orders given distinctly, concluded that it probably was not best to provoke us, and therefore quietly surrendered. To General Russell, who is one of the best and bravest officers in our service, belongs the credit of this brilliant success. He displayed one of the finest traits of generalship in selecting the time and mode of attack. The position in the daytime could only have been carried at a loss of at least fifteen hundred men. As it was, our loss did not exceed three hundred, and with a total result of four cannon, eight colors, sixteen hundred prisoners, and sixteen hundred stand of arms.

It is believed that a great battle is soon to be fought. Our army is in excellent condition, and will give a good account of itself.

Headquarters Second Brigade, November 21, 1863.

My dear Sister: We are now encamped on John Minor Botts's estate, not far from Brandy Station, where, perhaps, you will remember the

68

severe cavalry-fight took place last spring, before the opening of the Pennsylvania campaign.

John Minor Botts (1802 – 1869) was a nineteenth-century politician and lawyer from Virginia. He was jailed by the Confederates for pro-Unionist sentiments but refused to fight for the Union against Virginia.— Ed. 2016

Hazel River, a beautiful stream, runs close to our camp, and forms quite an obstacle should the enemy desire to turn our right. The troops have made themselves comfortable, but not with the conviction that they were to remain here very long. It is now storming, so whatever move may have been determined on will have to be delayed till the weather and the roads permit its execution. The general impression is, that a terrible battle is in store for us, but, far from wishing it deferred, the troops are, on the contrary, anxious for it. The army is in splendid spirits, well equipped, and confident. The success at the Rappahannock had a most electrifying-effect throughout the army, and I am sure, should we be maneuvered with skill, the enemy will meet with a crushing defeat.

The gallant conduct displayed by Upton at Rappahannock Station could not well be passed by unrewarded, and he was therefore selected to deliver to General Meade, commanding the Army of the Potomac, the battle-flags captured by the Second and Third Brigades. It is true that this appears but an empty honor compared with the gallant deeds which our hero had performed, but even such honors as these had their great value in the increased respect and admiration that were engendered in the breasts of his comrades. It is, perhaps, well here to comment upon the influences which the lack of just and fitting rewards to successful soldiers have upon the esprit de corps of the army.

Promotion on the field of battle is the only external reward that properly goes hand-in-hand with distinguished valor; and when true merit is for the time being overlooked, and the rewards are given to political favorites, zeal in the service, exposure in battle, and active interest, so essential for success, are not unfrequently replaced by lukewarmness and indifference. It reflects the highest credit upon Upton's personal and soldierly character when we find, in his private and personal letters to his relatives, no other than a just shade of discontent, without the slightest inclination to do other than his whole duty to the country, whether the reward to which he was clearly entitled came or not. To the true soldier higher position in rank brings higher responsibilities; and it cannot be doubted that in this gallant hero the animating spirit was far removed from selfish ambition, but he felt, rather, the power within him to do greater deeds of valor, with less sacrifice to the men confided to his care, than many others who were preferred before him on personal or political considerations. It is, therefore, eminently proper to insert these letters, written in confidence to his sister, and to substantiate their statements by the commendatory letters freely offered him by his commanders, who were gallant soldiers themselves, and fully acquainted with his conspicuous services:

Headquarters Second Brigade, April 10, 1864.

My dear Sister: My long-expected promotion is not forthcoming. General Meade has informed me that without "political" influence I will never be promoted. This consolation, however, remains, if justice has not been done, I have ever performed my duty faithfully and without regard to personal safety. The recommendation of those officers whose lives have been periled in every battle of the war have been overweighted by the baneful influence of the paltry politicians.... General Sedgwick has urged my claims, and stated that they were superior to those of any other in his corps, yet two colonels have been appointed over me.

Although the rank of a general may never be conferred on me, yet I hope to leave my friends abundant proof that I earned the honor, but that it was unjustly withheld. The spring campaign will soon be inaugurated. I trust General Grant will sustain his former reputation, and administer to General Lee such heavy blows that he may never recover. I confess I am ready for action, and I trust, in the coming struggle, we shall bear ourselves like men. The Army of the Potomac deserves a better name than it has, as we will soon prove. May God bless our arms, and grant us victory and peace!

Headquarters Second Brigade, April 18, 1864.

My dear Sister: There are considerable activity and preparation in the army for the coming campaign, and I think that officers and soldiers are anxious for marching orders. Camp-life has become very irksome, and we welcome any change that will break up its monotony. Excitement is the spice of a soldier's life, and all old troops hunger for it after having rested for a long time. I do not expect a battle before the first of May, perhaps the middle, but we all are convinced that either a most glorious or a most disastrous one awaits us.

I trust Grant may prove himself the general his reputation proclaims him, and that the fall of Richmond may prove the fall of the Confederacy. I have not fully despaired of receiving promotion, but I have despaired of receiving it in the manner honorable to a soldier. It is now solely the reward of political influence, and not of merit, and this when a government is fighting for its own existence.

Headquarters Second Brigade, April 25, 1864.

My dear Sister:... Your views as to my promotion reflect strongly your sisterly affection for me, and they in no little degree enable me to preserve my equanimity and peace of mind under the treatment I have received.

You must remember that to expose one's self simply to get promotion would be an unworthy act, and therefore, in the future as in the past, I must do my full duty with equal fearlessness. I have received of late many gratifying proofs of the confidence and esteem of both officers and men under my command, and not only in my command, but outside of it. The officers of the First Brigade of this division were nearly unanimous in recommending me for promotion, in the hope I might be assigned to that command. Considering that their lives to a great degree would be in my hands, especially in battle, and that no motive other than their safety and welfare could prompt such action, is it not the highest tribute men can pay me, that they should select me as their chosen leader in the hour of battle? The compliment is the more gratifying as coming from the New Jersey brigade, preferring me over every colonel from their State. The recommendation will not be forwarded, but it will serve to show the opinion of the officers of this division. Would the President consult the views of my superior officers, whose reputation depends upon my conduct to a certain degree, or those officers whose lives are in my hands in action, my promotion would not be withheld. I ought to have had it a year ago. Should anything befall me in the struggle about to ensue, my friends will not be permitted the slight satisfaction that I had risen to the rank of a general officer. But you shall never blush at my conduct. I shall do my duty faithfully, and I shall leave behind a record to which you can always refer with pride and satisfaction.... We are expecting to move soon. Our army is in fine condition, and I have no doubt that the bloodiest battle of the war will be fought in a few days. General Grant is well liked, and, as he is taking time to prepare his campaign, there is strong probability of his success.

General Upton remained in command of the Second Brigade in all the operations of the Army of the Potomac from Mine Run, November 26, 1863, to December 3, 1863, and participated in all of the preliminary movements and skirmishes previous to the inauguration of General Grant's overland campaign from the Rapidan in May, 1864. This campaign, the bloodiest of the whole war, was prosecuted with the utmost vigor, and will be ever memorable for the many stubborn contests, the great losses, the fatiguing marches, and the pertinacity with which Grant endeavored to outflank Lee, as well as the success of Lee in keeping his stubborn antagonist from accomplishing his purpose. Historic battles and heroic incidents crowd each other in a campaign during which the "troops literally fought all day and marched all night." Upton's brief and soldierly official report of the operations of his brigade may be taken as a typical account of this remarkable period, and for this reason it is inserted here without abridgment.

Battle of the Wilderness: May 5 – 7

Battle of Spotsylvania Courthouse: May 8 – May 21

Battle of Cold Harbor May 31 – June 12

Headquarters Second Brigade, First Division, Sixth Corps,
September 1, 1864.

Major Henry R. Dalton, Acting Assistant Adjutant-General, First Division, Sixth Corps.

Major: I have the honor to submit the following report of the operations of the Second Brigade, during the five epochs of the campaign of the Army of the Potomac, from the Rapidan to Petersburg: First Epoch.—The brigade broke camp near the Hazel River at 4 A. m., May 4, 1864, crossing the Rapidan at Germanna Ford, and camped on the plank-road two miles beyond.

May 5th, the march was resumed along the plank-road toward Wilderness Tavern. The brigade was thrown out on a dirt-road leading to Mine Run, to cover the right flank of the column while passing; shortly after it moved by the left flank, and formed in line on the left of the corps. About 11 a. m. orders were received to advance to the support of the Fifth Corps, then engaged with the enemy on the Orange Court-House pike, two miles from Wilderness Tavern.

The advance was made by the right of wings, it being impossible to march in line of battle on account of the dense pine and nearly impenetrable thickets which met us on every hand. After overcoming great difficulties on the march, connection was made with the right of the Fifth Corps. Lieutenant-Colonel Carroll, commanding Ninety-fifth Pennsylvania Volunteers, while riding a short distance in front of his regiment, came suddenly upon a group of the enemy, who fired upon him, killing him instantly. Two or three companies of his regiment, under Captains Boyd, Burns, and Lieutenant Gordon, immediately charged, gallantly carrying the hill on which the enemy was posted and capturing about thirty prisoners. The position, although two hundred yards in advance of the Fifth Corps line, was important to hold, and the line was accordingly established there. Shortly after, the Third Brigade connected on our right.

The woods in front and around our position had been set on fire by the enemy to prevent our advance. The ground had previously been fought over and was strewed with wounded of both sides, many of whom must have perished in the flames, as corpses were found partly consumed.

Colonel Penrose, commanding Fifteenth New Jersey Volunteers at that time, placed himself under my command, and remained with the brigade during the rest of the epoch. His regiment behaved under all circumstances with a steadiness indicative of the highest state of discipline.

May 6th the brigade was ordered to attack at daylight, but the order was countermanded; there was constant skirmishing during the day, but not serious.

About 7 p. m. Lieutenant-Colonel Duffy, Assistant Inspector-General, brought the order to send two regiments to the extreme right—that flank of the corps having been turned. The One Hundred and Twenty-first New York and the Ninety-fifth Pennsylvania were designated, and were led on by Lieutenant-Colonel Duffy at double-quick. While marching, they encountered a fire from the left. The dense undergrowth necessarily lengthened out the column, and at the same time large masses of men breaking through their ranks threw both regiments into unavoidable confusion. Portions of both regiments were promptly reformed at the rifle-pits near General Sedgwick's headquarters, then the extreme right, and held their position firmly. As soon as my horse could be brought after receiving the order, I started after the two regiments, leaving the remainder of the brigade under command of Colonel Penrose, but before I could reach them they had been broken. I succeeded in rallying about half of each and advanced at once. At every step, officers and men who were falling back stated that there were no troops in front or on the right, from which latter direction bullets were then coming. About three hundred yards to the rear was General Morris's brigade of the Third Division thrown back to meet the attack. I therefore moved the two regiments back and formed on his right. Fragments of other regiments were formed on my right, and two companies of the Ninety-fifth Pennsylvania were deployed as skirmishers. Finding out, shortly after dark, the position of the remainder of the regiments, they were united at the rifle-pits and still continued to hold the right of the line. Lieutenant-Colonel Olcott, commanding the One Hundred and Twenty-first New York, while his regiment was reforming, rode to the front to ascertain the position of affairs. He was discovered by the enemy and wounded in the forehead by a musket-ball, from the effect of which he fell from his horse insensible and was made prisoner. An able and gallant officer, his absence was felt throughout the entire campaign. Lieutenant Patterson, aide-de-camp, was wounded.

About 10 p. m., the brigade leading, the corps moved by the left flank to the pike, thence back to near Wilderness Tavern, where a position was taken between the pike and plank-road, and fortified on the morning of the 7th. The withdrawal from the front of the enemy, though but a few yards from his line, was accomplished successfully and without loss.

Second Epoch.—The brigade leading, the corps moved from Wilderness Tavern at 9.30 p. m. on the 7th, via Chancellorsville to Piney Branch Church, where half an hour was taken for breakfast. Resuming the march on the Spottsylvania road, it came up early in the afternoon with the Fifth Corps, then engaging the enemy. About 6.30 p. m. it was formed in a fourth line on the right of the road to support an attack, but, threatening demonstrations being made on our right flank, a change of front to our right and rear was executed about dusk. The brigade remained in this position during the night, connecting on the right with Ayres's brigade of the First Division, Fifth Corps. On the morning of the 9th it was relieved by Crawford's division of the Fifth Corps, moved to the left of the Spottsylvania road, took up position and fortified. During the day several casualties occurred from artillery-fire. On the afternoon of the 10th an assault was determined upon, and a column of twelve regiments was organized, the command of which was assigned to me.

The point of attack, which was shown me by Captain Mackenzie, of the United States Engineers, was at an angle of the enemy's works near the Scott House, about half a mile to the left of the Spottsylvania road.

The intrenchments were of a formidable character, with abatis in front and surmounted by heavy logs, underneath which were loop-holes for musketry. In the re-entrant to the right of the house was a battery with traverses between the guns; there were also traverses at intervals along the entire work. About a hundred yards to the rear was another line of works, partly completed, and occupied by a second line of battle. The position was in an open field, about two hundred yards from a pine-wood. A wood-road led from our position directly to the point of attack. The ground was looked over by General Russell and myself, and the regimental commanders were also required to see it, that they might understand the work before them.

The column of attack was formed in four lines of battle, four regiments being on the right and eight on the left of the road. The regiments on the right moved up the road by the right flank, those on the left by the left flank, each regiment lying down as soon as in position. The lines were arranged from right to left as follows:

First line, One Hundred and Twenty-first New York, Ninety-sixth Pennsylvania, and Fifth Maine; second line, Forty-ninth Pennsylvania, Sixth Maine, and Fifth Wisconsin; third line, Forty-third and Seventy-seventh New York and One Hundred and Nineteenth Pennsylvania; fourth line, Second, Fifth, and Sixth Vermont.

No commands were given in getting into position. The pieces of the first line were loaded and capped; those of the others were loaded but not capped; bayonets were fixed. The One Hundred and Twenty-first New York and Ninety-sixth Pennsylvania were instructed, as soon as the works were carried, to turn to the right and charge the battery. The Fifth Maine was to change front to the left, and open an enfilading fire to the left upon the enemy. The second line was to halt at the works, and open fire to the front if necessary. The third line was to lie down behind the second and await orders. The fourth line was to advance to the edge of the woods, lie down, and await the issue of the charge. Colonel Seaver, commanding it, was instructed that he might have to form line obliquely to the left, and open fire to cover the left flank of the column. All the officers were directed to repeat the command "Forward" constantly from the commencement of the charge till the works were carried. At ten minutes before 6 p. m. Captain Dalton brought me the order to attack as soon as the column was formed, and stated that the artillery would cease firing at 6 p m. Twenty minutes elapsed before all the preparations were completed, when, at the command, the lines rose, moved noiselessly to the edge of the wood, and, with a wild cheer and faces averted, rushed for the works. Through a terrible front and flank fire the column advanced, quickly gaining the parapet. Here occurred a deadly hand-to-hand conflict. The enemy, sitting in their pits, with pieces upright, loaded, and with bayonets fixed, ready to impale the first who should 5 leap over, absolutely refused to yield the ground. The first of our men who tried to surmount the works, fell, pierced through the head with musket-balls; others, seeing the fate of their comrades, held their pieces at arm's-length and fired downward; while others, poising their pieces vertically, hurled them down upon their enemies, pinning them to the ground.

Lieutenant Johnson, of the One Hundred and Twenty-first New York, received a bayonet-wound through the thigh. Private O'Donnell, Ninety-sixth Pennsylvania, was pinned to the parapet, but was rescued by his comrades. A private of the Fifth Maine, having bayoneted a rebel, was fired at by a captain, who, missing his aim, in turn shared the same fate; the brave man fell by a shot from a rebel lieutenant.

The struggle lasted but a few seconds. Numbers prevailed, and, like a resistless wave, the column poured over the works, quickly putting *hors-de-combat* those who resisted, and sending to the rear those who surrendered. Pressing forward, and expanding to the right and left, the second line of intrenchments, its line of battle, and the battery, fell into our hands. The column of assault had accomplished its task: the enemy's lines were completely broken, and an opening had been made for the division which was to have supported on our left, but it did not arrive. Re-enforcements arriving to the enemy, our front and both flanks were assailed. The impulsion of the charge being lost, nothing remained but to hold the ground. I accordingly directed the officers to form their men outside the works and open fire, and then rode back over the field to bring forward the Vermonters in the fourth line, but they had already mingled in the contest, and were fighting with a heroism which has ever characterized that elite brigade.

The Sixty-fifth New York had also marched gallantly to the support of its comrades, and was fighting stubbornly on the left. Night had arrived. Our position was three quarters of a mile in advance of the army, and, being without prospect of support, was untenable. Meeting General Russell at the edge of the wood, he gave me the order to withdraw. I wrote the order and sent it along the line by Captain Gorton, of the One Hundred and Twenty-first New York, in accordance with which, under cover of darkness, the works were evacuated, the regiments returning to their former camps.

Our loss in this assault was about one thousand in killed, wounded, and missing. The enemy lost at least one hundred in killed at the first intrenchments, while a much heavier loss was sustained in his efforts to regain them. We captured between ten and twelve hundred prisoners and several stands of colors. Captain Burhaus, Forty-third New York, had two stands of colors in his hands, and is supposed to have been killed while coming back from the second line of intrenchments. Many rebel prisoners were shot by their own men in passing to the rear over the open field. Our officers and men accomplished all that could be expected of brave men; they went forward with perfect confidence, fought with unflinching courage, and retired only upon the receipt of a written order after having expended the ammunition of their dead and wounded comrades.

May 11th, the brigade made some unimportant changes of position. Early on the 12th it moved with the division toward the right flank of the army, but to the left again at 7 a. m., arriving in rear of the Second Corps at 9.30 a. m. The right flank of this corps being threatened, General Russell directed me to move to the right at double-quick to support it. Before we could arrive, it gave way. As the Ninety-fifth reached an elevated point of the enemy's works, about six hundred yards to the right of the Lendrum House, it received a heavy volley from the second line of works. Seeing that the position was of vital importance to hold, and that all the troops had given way up to this point, I halted the Ninety-fifth Pennsylvania, faced it to the front, and caused it to lie down. Its left rested near the works connecting with the Second Corps, while its right refused lay behind a crest, oblique to the works. Had it given way, the whole line of intrenchments would have been recaptured, and the fruit of the morning's victory lost, but it held the ground till the Fifth Maine and the One Hundred and Twenty-first New York came to its support, while the Ninety-sixth Pennsylvania passed on its right. Shortly after the Third and Vermont brigades arrived, a section of Gillis's battery, Fifth United States Artillery, under Lieutenant Metcalf, came up and opened fire, but was immediately charged, and lost nearly every horse, driver, and cannonier.

The enemy charged up to his works within a hundred feet of the guns, but a well-directed fire from the infantry behind the crest prevented his further advance. At the point where our line diverged from the works the opposing lines came in contact; but neither would give ground, and for eighteen hours raged the most sanguinary conflict of the war. The point remained in our possession at the close of the struggle, and is known as the "Angle."

The brigade was relieved at 5.30 p. m. by Colonel McLaughlin, of the Second Corps. Captain Fish, Assistant-Adjutant-General of the brigade, was killed while gallantly performing his duty early in the action. He was a brave, zealous, patriotic officer, and had distinguished himself in every battle in which he had been engaged. Captain Lamont, of the Fifth Maine, the only one of seven captains who escaped in the assault of the 10th, was among the killed. I desire also to mention, though not in my brigade, Major Ellis, of the Forty-ninth New York, and Major Truefitt, of the One Hundred and Nineteenth Pennsylvania, who, by their gallant conduct, excited the admiration of all. The former received a wound from which he has since died; the latter was killed. The country can ill afford to lose two such officers.

After being relieved the brigade was held in reserve, and, after dark, was marched to the right of General Ricketts's line, near the position occupied on the 9th. At 12 p. m., on the 13th, the brigade leading, the division moved to the left, in rear of Burnside's corps, to near the Anderson House. On the morning of the 14th it was ordered to cross the Ny River, and seize Myer's Hill, to the left and front of the Fifth Corps. Before reaching the position it had been carried by the regulars, whom we relieved.

The brigade was reduced to less than eight hundred, and of these, three regiments, the Fifth Maine, One Hundred and Twenty-first New York, and Ninety-sixth Pennsylvania, were required to continue the picket-line from the Fifth Corps to the river, leaving the Ninety-fifth

Pennsylvania in reserve. I sent a dispatch to General Wright, through Captain Paine, signal-officer, that, if the position was to be held, another brigade was necessary; but it could not be spared, and two small regiments—the Second and Tenth New Jersey—were sent instead. A lookout was posted on top of the house with a field-glass to observe the enemy's movements. At the same time a breastwork of rails was thrown up in front of the house and out-buildings, there being no other means of fortifying at hand.

About two hundred and fifty yards to the front of the house was a wood, to the right of which, eight hundred yards distant, was a high hill. To the left of the house was a broad, open field, on the far edge of which could be seen squads of cavalry. About 4 p. m. the lookout discovered infantry skirmishers on the hill described.

Apprehensive that the enemy's sharp-shooters might occupy the point of woods nearest the house, Colonel Lessig was directed to move forward the Ninety-sixth and take possession. Two companies of the Second New Jersey were sent in support, and the remainder of the regiment sent forward to the works. Colonel Lessig had scarcely entered the wood before he encountered two brigades of infantry forming to charge our position. He immediately fell back, while at the same time the Ninety-fifth Pennsylvania and Tenth New Jersey were ordered forward. They were barely in position when the enemy's column emerged from the woods. Simultaneously cavalry, with a battery of horse-artillery, galloped on to the field to the left of the house, which opened fire, nearly enfilading our line. The enemy was received with a well-directed fire, which checked his advance, but, coming on in superior numbers, we were compelled to abandon the position.

Our loss in killed, wounded, and missing, was about one hundred. The enemy admitted a loss of one hundred and sixty-one killed and wounded. Lieutenant-Colonel Weibeck, of the Second New Jersey, a brave officer and thorough soldier, was killed. After dark, the position was reoccupied by our troops.

May 15th and 16th, the brigade remained at Myer's Hill. May 17th, at 8 p. m., it marched back to the Angle, arriving at 5 a. m. on the 18th, and returned to Myer's Hill the same evening. May 19th, it moved forward on Warren's left and fortified. At 10 p. m., the brigade leading, we marched across the Ny River, to meet Ewell's attack. On the morning of the 20th we relieved part of Birney's division, our right

79

resting on the Fredericksburg road. On the 21st, at 4 p. m., we returned to Myer's Hill, and on the same day the Second Connecticut Heavy Artillery was assigned to the brigade.

Third Epoch.—Marched from Myer's Hill at 10.30 p. m., May 21st, reached Guinea Station at 1.30 p. m., May 22d, and rested four hours. Crossed the Mattapony at 6.30 p. m., and camped at Lebanon Church. On the 23d, resumed the march, and camped near Jericho bridge, on the North Anna, at 12 p. m. The troops were much exhausted. On the 24th, crossed the North Anna at 6 a. m., and went into position on the left of Griffin's division. On the 25th, moved to the right, crossed the Virginia Central Railroad at Noel's Station, and destroyed half a mile of the track.

Fourth Epoch.—At 8 a. m., May 26th, recrossed the North Anna, and accompanied trains to Chesterfield Station, arriving at 2 p. m. Resumed the march at 8 p. m. toward Hanovertown, crossed the Pamunkey at 11 a. m., May 27th, having made twenty-seven miles since the previous evening. May 28th, moved up the river two miles to rejoin the Second and Third Divisions. May 29th, made reconnaissance to Hanover Court-House. May 30th, moved at daylight toward Richmond, and bivouacked near Atlee Station, seven miles from Mechanicsville. Marched at 1 a. m., June 1st, for Cold Harbor, arriving at 11 a. m.

At 5 p. m., the brigade connecting with Ricketts's division on the right and the Third Brigade on the left was formed in four lines, preparatory to an assault upon the enemy's intrenchments on the Richmond road. The guide was to be left. The Second Connecticut, under Colonel Kellogg, was drawn up in column by battalion, forming the front three lines. The Fifth Maine, Ninety-fifth and Ninety-sixth Pennsylvania, and One Hundred and Twenty-first New York, formed the fourth line.

At 6 p. m., General Ricketts advanced, and, no movement taking place on my left, I directed Colonel Kellogg to move forward; shortly after which Lieutenant-Colonel McMahon, assistant-adjutant-general of the corps, brought me the order to advance, without regard to the guide. The Second Connecticut, anxious to prove its courage, moved to the assault in beautiful order. Crossing an open field, it entered a pine-wood, passed down a gentle declivity, and up a slight, ascent. Here the charge was checked. For seventy feet in front of the works the trees had been felled, interlocking with each other, and barring all further advance. Two paths, several yards apart, and wide enough for four men to march abreast, led through the obstructions. Up these, to the foot of the works, the brave men rushed, but were swept away by a converging fire, unable to carry the intrenchments. I directed the men to lie down, and not to return the fire. Opposite the right of the regiment the works were carried, and several prisoners captured, among whom was Major McDonald, of a North Carolina regiment, who informed me that their flank had been turned. The regiment was then marched to the point gained, and, moving to the left, captured the point first attacked. In this position, without support on either flank, the Second Connecticut fought till 3 a. m., when the enemy fell back to a second line of works.

Colonel Kellogg, its brave and able commander, fell in the assault at the head of his command. The loss of the Second Connecticut was fifty-three killed, one hundred and eighty-seven wounded, and one hundred and forty-six missing; total, three hundred and eighty-six. June 3d, another assault was ordered, but, being deemed impracticable along our front, was not made. From the 3d to the 12th of June the brigade lay behind intrenchments. Nearly a constant fire was kept up by sharp-shooters, and but few casualties occurred. Lieutenant Gordon, of the Ninety-fifth Pennsylvania, aide-de-camp, was dangerously wounded in the head.

Fifth Epoch.—The brigade marched at 11 p. m., June 12th, toward the Chickahominy. June 13th, was detached to guard the artillery and trains; and then crossed the Chickahominy, at Jones's Bridge, and encamped. Resumed the march at 6 a. m., June 14th, and encamped near the James River at 11 a. m. June 17th, at I A. m., took transports at Wilson's Wharf; disembarked at Bermuda Hundred at 6 a. m.; and rejoined the corps near Point of Rocks.

June 18th, moved in front of the works at 1 a. m. to support the attack of two brigades upon Long-street's corps. The order of attack was countermanded, and the brigade returned to its former position. June 19th, marched at 5 a. m. for Petersburg; relieved Stannard's brigade, on the right, at 10 p. m.; and intrenched during the night.

June 21st, at 9 p. m., was relieved by Stannard's brigade, and marched across the Jerusalem plank-road to the left of the Second Corps.

June 22d, advanced with the Second Corps; met the enemy, but was not engaged. Captain R. S. Mackenzie, United States Engineers, commanding the Second Connecticut, was wounded. An attack was ordered at 7 p. m.; the line advanced, but the enemy had retired.

June 23d, several changes of position were made, and works were constructed near Williams's House. June 29th, at 3 p. m., marched to Reams's Station. June 30th, destroyed track, and returned to the Jerusalem plank-road. July 2d, returned to Williams's House. July 10th, marched to City Point, and took transports for Washington. The loss of the brigade during the campaign was three hundred and twenty-nine killed, seven hundred and thirteen wounded, and two hundred and sixty-three missing; total, fourteen hundred and five.

The officers and men endured the hardships of the campaign with remarkable patience, while the loss sustained sufficiently attests their gallantry. From the members of my staff—Captains J. D. Fish and F. G. Sanborn, and Lieutenants F. Morse, D. Gordon, and F. G. Patterson—I received, in every instance, prompt and gallant assistance.

Upton's report of the operations of his brigade may be taken as a typical one. Grant's overland campaign was really a continuous battle, from the passage of the Rapidan, May 4th, till the Army of the Potomac found itself intrenched in front of Petersburg. The terrible strain to which this gallant army had been subjected had almost reached the limit of human endurance.

General Humphreys well says: "The incessant movements, day and night, for so long a period; the constant, close contact with the enemy during all that time; the almost daily assaults upon intrenchments having entanglements in front, and defended by artillery and musketry in front and flank—exhausted officers and men. The larger part of the officers, who literally led their commands, were killed or wounded; and a large number of those that filled the ranks at the beginning of the campaign were absent. It is unreasonable to suppose that the troops were not, for a time, so exhausted as to need rest; and equally unreasonable to suppose that their opponents were not in a similar condition, though to a less degree, since they had not marched so much at night, nor attacked intrenchments."

See Humphrey's excellent The Virginia Campaign.—Ed. 2016

To this exhaustion we must, in a large measure, attribute the following criticism of General Upton upon the frequent assaults to which his troops had been ordered, found in a letter describing briefly the sequence of events, which are given in fuller detail in his report:

June 4, 1864.

My dear Sister:... I am disgusted with the generalship displayed. Our men have, in many instances, been foolishly and wantonly sacrificed. Assault after assault has been ordered upon the enemy's intrenchments, when they knew nothing about the strength or position of the enemy. Thousands of lives might have been spared by the exercise of a little skill; but, as it is, the courage of the poor men is expected to obviate all difficulties. I must confess that, so long as I see such incompetency, there is no grade in the army to which I do not aspire.

And again he writes:

Headquarters Second Brigade, June 5, 1864.

My dear Sister: We are now at Cold Harbor, where we have been since June 1st. On that day we had a murderous engagement. I say murderous, because we were recklessly ordered to assault the enemy's intrenchments, knowing neither their strength nor position. Our loss was very heavy, and to no purpose. Our men are brave, but cannot accomplish impossibilities. My brigade lost about three hundred men. My horse was killed, but I escaped unharmed. Since June 1st we have been behind rifle-pits, about three hundred yards from the enemy. A constant fusillade from both sides has been kept up, and, though but little damage has been done, it is, nevertheless, very annoying.

I am very sorry to say I have seen but little generalship during the campaign. Some of our corps commanders are not fit to be corporals. Lazy and indolent, they will not even ride along their lines; yet, without hesitancy, they will order us to attack the enemy, no matter what their position or numbers. Twenty thousand of our killed and wounded should today be in our ranks. But I will cease fault-finding, and express the hope that mere numbers will yet enable us to enter Richmond. Please give my love to all. I am as anxious to hear from home as you are to hear from me. The fatigue of the campaign hardly disposes one for letter-writing.

The severe character of these bloody contests can hardly be appreciated by those who were not themselves actors in the events described.

At the battle of the "Angle," [Spotsylvania] so continuous was the firing, that an oak-tree, over eighteen inches in diameter, was entirely cut in two by the bullets fired from the Union lines. A section of the remaining stump was afterward obtained and sent to Washington, which exhibits in a striking way the persistent struggle in which both the enemy and our own men engaged at this point.

The following letter gives a fuller account of this action, and is, therefore, inserted:

Fort Monroe, August 31, 1878.

To G. Norton Galloway, Esq.,

Philadelphia.

Dear Sir: On the morning of that day, the Sixth Corps was in rear of the right of the army, but, on receipt of the news that Hancock's corps had captured several thousand prisoners, and a large portion of the works in the vicinity of the Lendrum House, it was ordered to that point as a support. Our brigade was at the rear of the corps, and, when the corps got into position, occupied the right of the line. The brigade had scarcely halted when I received orders to move, in double time, to the support of the right of the Second Corps. Starting the brigade in double time, the Ninety-fifth Pennsylvania leading, I galloped to the crest at the "Angle," and from thence could see the right of our troops extending along the works, to the point where the twelve regiments of our corps made the assault on the 10th. I could also see a second line of works, the same we encountered and captured on the 10th, about one hundred or one hundred and fifty yards in front of the line then in our possession. This second line appeared to be unoccupied. After reconnoitering the position, I rode back to the head of the Ninety-fifth, ordered it to take a steady step, and then conducted it to the crest, intending to pass over it, and move on to the right of the line. But, on arriving at the crest, I saw that the flank of the troops had been turned, and that they had been compelled to abandon the intrenchments to the point where I then stood. A moment after, as the head of the Ninety-fifth, still marching in double time, crowned the crest, it received the full fire of a line of battle, occupying the second line of works already referred to. Instead of attempting to go over the crest, the head of the

84

regiment inclined to the right, then followed the crest until the left, or rear, rested on the works, when I caused the men to lie down and open fire. Had the regiment given way, there can be little doubt that the fruits of the gallant charge of the Second Corps in the morning would have been lost. But, in a few moments, the One Hundred and Twenty-first New York, the Ninety-sixth Pennsylvania, and the Fifth Maine came to its support, while the Jersey Brigade passed into the works on its right. Shortly after, the whole of the First Division, Sixth Corps, was engaged at the "Angle," and, immediately to its left, our right.

At the point where our line diverged from the works, the Union and Confederate soldiers were face to face. A few yards to the enemy's left (our right) of this point were the traverses of a four-gun battery, which had been captured in the morning.

It was from between those traverses, which proved a charnel-house to the Confederates, that they kept up a more or less continuous fire during the day, and, as I was informed, till nearly three o'clock next morning, when they abandoned the position. The tree was not the only evidence of the amount and accuracy of our fire. The top Jogs of the works and the traverses were splintered like brush-brooms, while the oak abatis in front was completely shot away. From 9.30 a. m. till about 5.30 p. m., when our brigade was relieved, these traverses were immediately in our front, and in front of the other brigades of the Sixth Corps, which came to our support. To our left, the troops of the Second Corps poured in an oblique fire toward the traverses. It was thus from the front fire of the Sixth Corps, aided by an oblique fire of the Second Corps, that the tree was undoubtedly shot down.

The "Angle" was first captured by the Second Corps, and, during the prolonged conflict of nearly eighteen hours, was held chiefly by the Sixth Corps. A few days after the battle, Major-General Birney, of the Second Corps, volunteered the information to me that, in his official report, he would give our brigade the credit of saving the day.

Such conspicuous gallantry could not be passed without official notice. Upton's commanding officers, unsolicited, gave the strongest indorsements of his fitness for a higher command, and his promotion to the grade of brigadier-general was not long delayed. These recommendations are worthy of preservation in this record, not only on account of the merit they extol, but because of the soldierly generosity of his immediate superiors.

General Joseph J. Bartlett, commanding the Second Brigade of the First Division, Sixth Corps, says:

"Colonel Upton's services in the field date from the first battles before Manassas, as aide-de-camp to Brigadier-General Tyler. Subsequently he was assigned to Battery D, Second United States Artillery, which he commanded at West Point, Virginia, May 7, 1862. At the battles at Gaines's Mills and Charles City Cross-roads he commanded his battery with great skill and gallantry. At the battles of Crampton's Gap and Antietam he commanded an artillery brigade of twenty-six guns.

"October 25, 1862, he was promoted colonel of the One Hundred and Twenty-first New York Volunteers. In the subsequent battles of the Army of the Potomac he commanded his regiment with distinguished ability, and has received honorable mention in all of my reports, and in the reports of the division commanders.

"Colonel Upton's conduct in the field has been marked by a prompt and cheerful obedience to orders, and an untiring endeavor to elevate his command to its greatest efficiency. His unswerving integrity, his skill in the management of his regiment in action, his coolness and bravery under fire, have won for him the respect of his comrades and superior officers.

"The promotion of Colonel Upton would be but an act of justice, in consideration of his services, and would at the same time secure in the position of brigadier-general a faithful, conscientious, and reliable commander."

The foregoing letter was indorsed as follows:

"Colonel Upton, who is an officer of the regular army, has served either as commander of his regiment or of the Second Brigade of this division, since my connection with the Army of the Potomac; and, by the zeal, intelligence, energy, and gallantry he has uniformly exhibited, has shown himself fully competent for the position for which he has been recommended. I not only take pleasure in presenting his claims for promotion on the record within, but would urge his appointment on the higher ground of the interest of the service.

"H. G. Wright,

"Brigadier-General commanding First Division, Sixth Corps."

"Colonel Upton has taken part, either as battery, regimental, or brigade commander, in all the battles in which this corps has been engaged, and has rendered gallant and important service. At Crampton's Pass and Antietam he was chief of artillery of the corps. In the battles at and near Fredericksburg, in December and May last, he commanded his regiment; and at Gettysburg, and for some time subsequent, he was in command of a brigade. On all these occurrences his conduct was admirable. His regiment is in a highly efficient state of discipline. Colonel Upton would make an excellent brigade commander, and I earnestly hope he may be appointed.

"John Sedgwick,

"Major-General commanding Sixth Corps"

General "Uncle John" Sedgwick was one of the most dependable commanders in the Union army. He was killed on May 9, 1864 at the Battle of Spotsylvania Courthouse. His last words as he walked along the Union lines were, "What? Men dodging this way for single bullets? What will you do when they open fire along the whole line? Why are you dodging like this? They couldn't hit an elephant at this distance." When informed of Sedgwick's death, General Grant repeatedly asked, "Is he really dead?"—Ed. 2016

"I fully concur in the foregoing recommendations, and trust that, in consideration of the high qualifications Colonel Upton possesses for the position, as well as on account of the distinguished and gallant services he has rendered during the war, he will receive the appointment of brigadier-general.

"George G. Meade,

"Major-General commanding."

Numerous other attestations of his eminent services are at hand, and could be printed were they necessary, to exhibit the strong impression that he made upon those with whom he served.

The care which he bestowed upon his men, the high state of discipline to which he brought his command, the deliberate study which he made of the positions he was directed to assault, the ample provision he made for every contingency, the cool daring, gallant bearing, and remarkable success which always attended his going into action, all combined to make him a hero to his soldiers, and an illustrious example to his brother officers. There was no jealousy excited when his promotion followed, for it was given for "gallant and distinguished services," well earned, as his comrades knew.

Headquarters Second Brigade, June 7, 1864.

My DEAR Sister:... I first saw my promotion in the papers on June 1st. I was very glad; for, two hours after, as I wrote you, we went into action. I am disposed to think that it will be better in the end for me to have received my promotion at this late date. The reasons for my promotion are gratifying to any soldier. It will be entered upon the records of the War Department that I was promoted for "gallant and distinguished services"—a record that will help me through life, and one of which you will be far more proud than had it been conferred simply for political reasons. It is contrary to the instincts of all regular officers to seek promotion through the latter influence. Everybody congratulates me, and all concede that I have fairly earned it; even those who have opposed me acknowledge this. I feel quite happy, and have not yet ceased to aspire. I shall not be content until I get a division, and time will bring that about. My health has been remarkably good throughout the campaign. I have slept in my clothes, with the exception of two or three nights, since May 4th, and the same has been done by nearly all the officers and men.

Headquarters Second Brigade, June 18, 1864.

To-night I am quietly writing in my tent, which was last pitched on the north bank of the James. We took transports yesterday morning at 1 a. m., and steamed up to Bermuda Hundreds, arriving there at 6 a. m. Thence we marched to Point of Rocks, on the Appomattox. This morning we were marched outside of the works to support and participate in an assault upon the enemy's works. The order was countermanded in time to prevent a deliberate murder of our troops. The line we were to assault was evacuated by the enemy on the 16th, and was occupied by our troops, who fell back from them without firing a shot. It was not till the enemy had reoccupied them in stronger force than before that it was discovered that their possession was of great importance to us. Brilliant generalship that, which would abandon voluntarily a line of works, allow the enemy to take possession, and then drive them from it by a glorious charge This kind of stupidity has cost us already twenty thousand men. It is time that it should be stopped. I think, however, with all our stupid blunders in battle, we shall yet succeed. To all intents and purposes, we hold Petersburg. Our cavalry should cut the Lynchburg Canal and the Danville Railroad, which will certainly necessitate the evacuation of Richmond. There has been, I judge, terrible fighting today at Petersburg, but I do not know the result. It must have been in our favor, I think, otherwise we would have been ordered to re-enforce the corps engaged. Our corps is at present under the orders of General Butler, but we hope soon to join the Army of the Potomac.

The arduous struggle for the possession of Richmond, which commenced with the movement of the Army of the Potomac across the Rapidan on the 4th of May, 1864, had for the time being ceased. The theatre of operations was peculiarly well fitted for the defensive measures which General Lee so ably conducted, and was correspondingly difficult for the offensive operations undertaken by General Grant. The task of the former was to prevent the penetration of the Union forces between his army and Richmond, and to secure always the shortest line of retreat to Richmond, and the safety of his line of supplies. That of the latter was to bring the enemy to battle in the open field, or, by rapid flank movements or overwhelming assaults, to dislodge him from his defensive positions, keeping Washington always well covered in his rear.

The southeasterly trend of the various streams having their sources in the Blue Ridge offered a succession of strong positions to the enemy, and which, by Lee's able generalship, proved insurmountable barriers to a direct overland march of Grant's forces.

During the progress of the campaign secondary expeditions were devised, having for their purpose the detaching of sufficiently strong portions of the enemy's troops, so as to weaken him, and enable the Army of the Potomac to accomplish more readily its purpose.

General Hunter's command in the Shenandoah Valley had gained such success in his Lynchburg campaign while the two main opposing forces were struggling at the North Anna, that Lee was constrained to send back to the Valley two brigades commanded by Breckenridge. This force was further increased by the addition of Early's corps, withdrawn from Lee's forces June 13th, after the issue at Cold Harbor had been decided in favor of Lee. The result of these movements was to drive Hunter out of the Shenandoah toward the Kanawha Valley. He reached Charleston, West Virginia, June 30th, with his troops foot-sore and exhausted, and was thus eliminated as a factor of offense or defense in the Shenandoah until near the middle of July. The situation was now something like this: Grant was moving his forces south to invest Petersburg, and, crossing his army over the James River at and near Fort Powhatan, but covering his real movement by a portion of his cavalry near Malvern Hill and White-Oak Swamp. Lee, watchful, was waiting for information as to Grant's movements, but ready to interpose in his front, either south of Richmond or Petersburg. Early, in the Valley, with nothing of any moment to oppose him, had an inviting pathway into Maryland. His force, of about seventeen thousand men, mostly veteran troops, was strong enough not only to penetrate into Maryland, but to seriously threaten and endanger Washington. Lee hoped by this diversion to cause Grant to loosen the powerful grasp by which he held the bulk of his forces in the intrenchments around Petersburg.

Briefly, it may be stated that Early, in the prosecution of this design, reached Winchester July 2d, entered Hagerstown, Md., on the 6th, and, after terrifying all Maryland, appeared in sight of Washington on the nth. The near presence of this veteran force to Washington caused the greatest consternation. To oppose it there were only some convalescents, some raw and untried troops, and the civilian employees of the Quartermaster's Department, and Grant was urged to send a sufficient force from the Army of the Potomac to avert the danger.

On the night of the 9th of July, orders were sent to General Wright, commanding the Sixth Corps, to march the First and Second Divisions of this corps from their camps at Petersburg to City Point, there to take transports for Washington. Embarking at daylight, they were landed at Washington on the afternoon of the nth, in time to oppose any serious attack of Early. On the 12th,

Early's attack was defeated, and his retreat to the Shenandoah began. He was followed by General Wright, who was at first inferior to Early in strength, and hence was compelled, from prudential motives, to move with some caution. The arrival of Hunter's forces in the vicinity of Harper's Ferry aided in causing the retreat of Early ultimately to Strasburg. On the 23d of July the Sixth Corps was withdrawn to Washington with the intention of sending it back to the Army of the Potomac; but the enemy, ever watchful, took advantage of this withdrawal and, by an advance movement, succeeded in defeating General Crook at Kernstown, in the Valley, which had the effect of bringing back the Sixth Corps to Harper's Ferry.

On the 24th of July the Confederate cavalry under McCausland began a new raid into Maryland, the same day that Crook's forces united with the Sixth Corps at Harper's Ferry. Chambersburg, in Pennsylvania, was burned; stores, provisions, and horses were captured, and another stampede among the farmers of Maryland and Southern Pennsylvania occurred. Grant determined to put a stop forever to this disturbing element of his main purpose, and, as a result, the army in the Valley was re-enforced and General Sheridan was sent to command it. He was to defeat and disperse Early's forces, and make such a destruction of all the resources of the Shenandoah Valley as to prevent in future any possibility of the subsistence of the enemy's forces in that locality.

General Upton, commanding his brigade in the First Division of the Sixth Corps, took part in all the movements which resulted from the operations of Early referred to above, and in the following letters gives a brief account of what came under his notice:

Snicker's Gap, July 19, 1864.

My dear Sister:... We have had a bloodless campaign since the rebels invaded Maryland. The timely arrival of our corps saved Washington from capture. The enemy withdrew from the city and made a hasty retreat across the Potomac. We have followed leisurely and without opposition until reaching this point. We are encamped on the west side of the Blue Ridge, and hold the east bank of the Shenandoah, while the enemy holds the west bank. I wish you could enjoy this scenery. From our camp on the Blue Ridge the Great Valley of Virginia, with its surrounding streams, its groves, its fertile fields, and elegant mansions, is spread out like a beautiful landscape. Seldom does the tourist meet with a view so enchanting. A glance of the eye comprehends the Blue Ridge, the Alleghanies, Maryland Heights, and innumerable smaller mountains dotted here and there throughout the Valley, 6 lending additional charms to the scenery. I do not know where this war may lead us before its close. I certainly did not expect to visit this region with a portion of the Army of the Potomac.

Headquarters Second Brigade, Harper's Ferry, August 9, 1864.

My dear Sister: A new campaign will be inaugurated tomorrow under the command of General Sheridan. How soon it may develop the enemy, and what may be its consequences no one knows, but I trust it will be successful. General Sheridan has the appearance of great nerve, and hitherto has been quite successful. For one, I am better pleased with his appearance than that of any other commander under whom I have served. How humiliating was the reverse at Petersburg, and how disgraceful on the part of division commanders to abandon their troops! I have never been reckless, but I am sure it is a praiseworthy quality when so few of our higher commanders expose themselves as much as duty requires. It has now arrived at that point when officers must expose themselves freely if they would have their commands do their whole duty; so, whatever I may do, you must not attribute it to rashness, but to a soldier's sense of duty.

Harper's Ferry, August 24, 1864,

My dear Sister: I would like very much to spend Saturday and Sunday, September 9th and 10th, at home, but do not look forward to such an event. Our movements depend upon Early, who is a contrary fellow, and may give us much trouble about that time. Everything considered, I am not justified in allowing you to look forward, as the chances against the realization of our wish are nine out of ten. I will telegraph in time to let you know.

We had quite a skirmish with the enemy last Sunday. I was on the skirmish-line and received repeated hints from the rebels that my presence was obnoxious, but, as their practice was bad, I escaped unhurt.

Charlestown, Va., September 2, 1864.

My dear Sister: We expect to move tomorrow morning up the Valley. This, unfortunately, I fear, banishes all hope of returning home. I am, however, willing to forego all pleasure if for the good of the country. The impression is very strong that Early is en route to Richmond; if so, your brother may soon date his letters from Petersburg. I am in good spirits over both military and political prospects. The rebels cannot disguise the fact that their power is on the wane, and that their race is nearly run. While the nomination of McClellan on so damnable a platform renders Lincoln's re-election certain, I am out and out for Lincoln. He has made many gross blunders, but he is true to his purpose, and, when the South, after four years of war, finds that the North is as determined as ever to crush the rebellion, the rebellion will collapse. [Admiral David] Farragut is a hero, and deserves all the honors a grateful nation can bestow. Grant, too, is rising daily in the opinion of the officers who were ill-affected toward him when he took command. Others that I could mention are stumbling-blocks of too great magnitude to permit a brilliant execution of any movement in which they may be implicated. I heartily wish they might be relieved.

Sheridan's forces in the Valley were obliged at first to act on the defensive, because of the reinforcements which Early had received. It was, nevertheless, believed that in due time the necessities of Lee would bring about the recall of a large portion, if not the whole, of the Confederate force now confronting Sheridan. The latter, ever on the alert, hoped to overwhelm the diminished force of the enemy when such an event took place, and, to better arrange for this, he had established himself, in the early part of September, in the vicinity of Berryville, in a strong position, threatening Winchester, and having the fine defensive position at Halltown to fall back upon in case the enemy pressed him too closely. On the 14th of September, the main part of the re-enforcements (Kershaw's division) which Early had received were finally recalled to join Lee's army at Richmond. Early also, at this juncture, separated his forces, sending a large part to Martinsburg, on the Baltimore and Ohio Railroad, twenty-two miles north of Winchester.

Sheridan, quickly taking advantage of these two circumstances, concentrated his forces on the Opequan, near Winchester, and moved directly against Ramseur's division, covering that place. The battle took place on the 19th of September, and resulted in a marked victory for Sheridan. The part played by Upton in this action was, as usual, conspicuous. At first in command of his brigade, with which he was the first, after Wilson's division of cavalry, to arrive on the field, the death of General Russell gave him the command of the First Division. This division was, in the early part of the engagement, held in reserve in rear of the right of the Sixth Corps. The advance of this corps was along the Winchester and Berryville pikes—Getty, with the Second Division, on the left, and Ricketts, with the Third Division, on the right; the Nineteenth Corps was on the right of the Sixth Corps, and connected with it during the first advance, until about midday. Due to the change of direction of the Berryville pike toward the left, an interval occurred between the right of the Sixth Corps and the left of the Nineteenth, which increased in width as the troops advanced. The enemy, taking advantage of this, pushed in Battle's brigade of Rhodes's division, which, being supported by the other brigades of this division and that of Gordon, drove back Ricketts's division of the Sixth Corps and Grover's of the Nineteenth Corps. This, for a short time, not only checked the Union advance, but forced back the whole line some distance. "At this juncture Russell's division of the Sixth Corps splendidly improved a golden opportunity. Ordered at once to move up into the front line, now needing re-enforcement, this change brought it into the gap created by the Confederate charge, and, continuing its advance, it struck the flank of the hostile force which was sweeping away the Union right, and, aided by the Fifth Maine Battery, which enfiladed the enemy's line with canister, at once turned the tide. The enemy retreated, the line was re-established, the fugitives were gathered from the woods in which they had taken refuge, while the gallant division took position on the right of its corps. But, in the hour of his triumph, Russell had fallen. 'His death,' said Sheridan, 'brought sadness to every heart in the army.' The broken portion of Ricketts's line was quickly reformed behind the First Division, now under Upton, and again moved forward, while Dwight's division, having taken the place of Grover's, on the right of the line, the latter was promptly rallied and brought up." The report of the operations of the division was made by Major Dalton, assistant-adjutant-general. "The enemy," he says, "having

94

pushed back the Second Division of the Nineteenth Corps, and a portion of the Third Division of this corps, moved down toward the pike, delivering a severe fire of musketry from the woods and corn-fields on the right. The Third Brigade (Edwards's) was now rapidly moved by the flank to the right of the pike, then forward with the First Brigade (Campbell's) under a heavy fire to a crest commanding the woods and fields through which the enemy moved. This advance was very much assisted by the First New York Battery, commanded by Lieutenant Johnson, which did splendid execution, and was fought with gallantry under a very annoying musketry-fire. At this time, General Upton moved his brigade into line to the right of the pike, at an oblique angle to it, thence forward into the woods, delivering heavy volleys into masses of the enemy, who were coming up. This fresh fire from the Second Brigade (Upton's) soon caused the enemy to fall back, so that the whole line moved forward to a position which was easily held till the latter part of the afternoon, though occasionally sharp musketry-fire was interchanged. While personally superintending the advance of the First and Third Brigades to the crest previously referred to, and which he considered of the utmost importance, General Russell was killed by a piece of shell which passed through his heart—he had just before received a bullet-wound in the left breast, but had not mentioned this to any of his staff, continuing to urge forward his troops."

General Upton's account is as follows:

"After marching about half a mile, the troops on the right of the pike gave way; line was immediately formed, and soon after. Lieutenant-Colonel Kent gave me the order to move the brigade to the right. The brigade was faced to the right, and marched across the pike into a narrow belt of timber, where the second line was halted and faced to the front. The Second Connecticut continued the march, inclining to the right, making our line oblique to that upon which the enemy was advancing. Bayonets were fixed, and instructions given not to fire till within close range. The enemy's left, extending far beyond our right, advanced till within two hundred yards of our line, when a brisk flank-fire was opened by the One Hundred and Twenty-first and Sixty-fifth New York, causing him to retire in great disorder. The whole line then advanced, driving the enemy, and inflicting a heavy loss in the killed and wounded. The brigade was halted at the edge of the wood, which

95

position it held till the attack was renewed in the afternoon. On the left of the brigade the Thirty-seventh Massachusetts rendered invaluable service in supporting Stevens's Fifth Maine Battery."

General [George] Crook, who commanded the Army of Western Virginia, known afterward as the Eighth Corps, says, in his report of the battle: "The general direction of my line was on the enemy's left flank, and at right angles to the line of the Nineteenth Corps. During the latter part of the charge there was a succession of stone fences running parallel to my lines, behind which some of the flying enemy took refuge, pouring a destructive fire into my ranks. On riding to the Nineteenth Corps to request them to enfilade these fences, I found Brigadier-General Upton, of the Sixth Corps, on my left, making a most gallant charge with the brigade against the enemy thus posted, although having been in the hottest of the fight since its commencement in the morning. Finally, the enemy fled from these fences, pursued through the town of Winchester by my command, which was the first to enter the city."

It appears, from the various accounts, that the timely arrival of Upton's brigade upon the field of battle, and its vigorous attack upon the advancing enemy in the gap between the right of the Sixth and left of the Nineteenth Corps, were most opportune. It turned a possible defeat into certain victory. General Upton was severely wounded in the right thigh near the close of the battle, but with the nerve and coolness of the true soldier he remained until the action was over, although directed by General Sheridan to quit the field. It is related that, not being able, on account of his wound, to remain on his horse, he had a stretcher borne by a detachment of the ambulance corps, and in this was carried along the line from place to place, encouraging his men and giving his orders with a courage and devotion full of inspiration to his troops. The fortitude thus displayed is worthy of a true hero, and stands in noticeable contrast to the retirement from the field of others only slightly wounded.

The severe nature of his wound caused him, two days after the battle, to take a leave of absence, and, proceeding to his home, he awaited with impatience its healing sufficiently to allow his return to active duty. For his services in this battle he was brevetted a major-general of volunteers.

DIVISION COMMANDER OF CAVALRY

In October, 1864, the returns of the cavalry of the Military Division of the Mississippi showed a nominal strength of nearly eighty thousand men, only fourteen thousand of whom were actually fit for duty in the field. This large force was unavailable for the more important duties of cavalry, because it was scattered over the States of Kentucky, Missouri, Tennessee, Alabama, and Georgia, in detachments of various strength, and was without unity, either in command, purpose, discipline, or organization. This arm of the service had naturally suffered from defective organization and hard service, and had therefore failed to develop the proper morale and military spirit. But both General Grant and General Sherman believed that, with a proper organization and a competent leader, it could attain a standard of excellence equal to the cavalry of the Army of the Potomac, which would make it a most potent factor in a campaign directed toward the heart of the Confederacy, and which had not yet been touched.

General James H. Wilson [author of the introduction to this volume], then commanding a division with Sheridan in the Valley of Virginia, was detailed by General Grant, and ordered to report to Sherman for the purpose of reorganizing and commanding the Western cavalry. He was promised the assistance of a few good brigade and division commanders from the Army of the Potomac, and requested that Upton, among others, might be ordered to join him. This request was granted, although the latter had not yet recovered from the severe and painful wound received at the battle of Winchester, and could not again take the field till late in December. It will be remembered that up to this time Upton had served only with the artillery and infantry, but so thoroughly had his qualities become known throughout the army that neither General Grant nor his new commander had any doubt about his success as a cavalry leader. Indeed, his enterprise, intrepidity, and general ability had specially marked him as one of the best officers in the army for the duty of assisting in bringing the mounted service up to the high degree of discipline and efficiency which all arms had reached in the Eastern armies, and which both the artillery and infantry had

98

reached in the Western armies. In order that his services in the West may be better understood, we may briefly refer to a few of the salient facts connected with the cavalry commands in the Military Division of the Mississippi at this epoch.

Three divisions of cavalry, about five thousand in the aggregate, commanded by Generals McCook, Garrard, and Kilpatrick, were attached to the Army of the Cumberland. In the Army of the Ohio the cavalry consisted of a portion of a division near Atlanta under General Garrard, while Capron's brigade was awaiting a remount at Louisville, Kentucky, all under the command of General George Stone-man. There were two divisions of cavalry belonging to the Army of the Tennessee, one in West Tennessee, under General Edward Hatch, and the other in Missouri and Tennessee, near Memphis, under Colonel E. F. Winslow, Fourth Iowa Cavalry—the whole commanded by Brigadier-General B. H. Grierson. Many detachments, employed as escorts, foragers, orderlies, hospital attendants, etc., were to be found in all the armies. In addition to the above, a few regiments of good cavalry and a division of mounted infantry were located in Kentucky and East Tennessee. There were in all about eighty-two regiments of mounted troops, or rated as such, spread over a wide territory, partially paralyzed, at least, by the scattering policy to which this arm of the service had been subjected.

Although General Sherman expressed no great faith in the views and plans of General Wilson, or in the possibility of their practical application within the limits of the time available, he cordially consented to their adoption, and frankly said he would not undertake to divide the honors which the reorganized cavalry might gain for its new commander. He accordingly issued the order constituting these widely scattered and fragmentary bodies into the Cavalry Corps of the Military Division of the Mississippi, under the command of General Wilson. This order was issued at Gaylesville, Alabama, on the 9th of November, 1864, and, while it marked a great epoch in the history of the cavalry in the West, much had yet to be done to make the corps in effect something more than a mere name. The organization consisted of seven divisions, commanded by

Generals McCook, Long, Kilpatrick, Grierson, Hatch, Johnson, and Knipe, respectively.

The Third Division (Kilpatrick's), having been selected to accompany General Sherman in his march to the sea, had been strengthened by the absorption of nearly all the good horses left with the army, and by bringing forward the detached men who were guarding railroads and block-houses; the strength of its three brigades was thus increased to about five thousand men for duty. The dismounted divisions were sent back to Louisville for remounts, and it was hoped that this could be effected in time to make use of them in the operations against Hood. By the 14th of November Wilson had a force of eight thousand mounted and two thousand unmounted men, and did employ them with vigor and effect in the decisive battle of Nashville, December 15th and 16th, although but a short time had elapsed since this force was without cohesion or military value.

During the pursuit of Hood the cavalry captured thirty-two guns, eleven caissons, twelve colors, three thousand two hundred and thirty prisoners, and caused the abandonment or destruction of many wagons, horses, and mules, belonging to Hood's army.

It had been General Grant's design that an active winter campaign into Alabama should immediately follow the defeat of Hood, and it was expected that the initiative would be made about the latter part of December. But many causes united to greatly modify the original plan and somewhat delay the contemplated movement, so that it finally resulted in a campaign by the cavalry corps itself, beginning in the latter part of March.

Wilson had been directed to assemble his cavalry, after Hood's defeat, in the vicinity of Huntsville, Alabama. But, because of the impoverished state of the country, due to its having been overrun by the forces of both parties, and because of the lack of railroad facilities for the supply of large bodies of troops, headquarters were established at Gravelly Springs, fifteen miles below Florence, on the Tennessee River, and the command was collected in cantonments between that place and Waterloo. During February and early March, all the divisions of the corps (except the Third, which had accompanied Sherman in his march to the sea) had arrived and were placed in camp. Every effort was made to drill and discipline these troops, so that they would form a coherent and reliable body of horse.

Thorough amalgamation was impossible during the retreat before Hood from the Tennessee to the Cumberland, or during the preparation for the battle of Nashville. Then during the pursuit of Hood the troops and horses had been severely pushed, and their powers of endurance nearly exhausted, and yet, while their spirits had been raised by their successes during the battle and subsequent pursuit, the discipline had suffered in some degree. Roll-calls had been neglected, and many essential military duties had been perfunctorily performed. As soon as the command was assembled on the Tennessee, the corps commander, aided by a large and an efficient staff, set himself to correct these shortcomings, and soon had the pleasure of seeing unsoldierly conduct and all irregularity replaced by a prompt and willing obedience and the strictest discipline. Both men and horses were comfortably sheltered and supplied. They were drilled at every opportune moment, and soon there grew up an organized body of horse capable of efficient employment. The difficulties which, at first, seemed almost insurmountable, had been gradually dissipated, till finally everything was in readiness for a campaign into the very heart of the South. But the rainy weather of March had filled the Tennessee till its banks and bottom-lands were flooded; the roads were in a frightful condition, and that part of the country which was not a quagmire was a barren waste. For ninety miles south of the Tennessee the country had been completely stripped of all supplies, and hence it was necessary to accumulate food, forage, and munitions of all kinds, so that the command could move out at the earliest moment that the roads would permit. The aggregate force with which the corps was expected to penetrate the enemy's territory was twenty-five thousand men. But orders in February directed that one division be sent to Canby, operating at Mobile; one division be left at Chickasaw to watch the Mississippi and Tennessee Rivers; and one be detached for service in Tennessee. The Seventh Division, General Knipe, was selected for the first detail; the Fifth, General

Hatch, for the second; and the Sixth, General Johnson, for the last—in all about ten thousand troopers.

General Wilson was left with about fourteen thousand men, of whom fifteen hundred were not mounted, to undertake his campaign in a new and untried territory against an active cavalry force of the enemy, commanded by one of its most prominent cavalry leaders, General Forrest.

We will now see how General Upton became connected with the operations which followed. Severely wounded at the battle of Winchester, in Virginia, October 19, 1864, he was thereby prevented from immediately joining his new command. He had played so conspicuous a part in this battle, and his bravery and military ability were so marked, that the Government promptly rewarded him with the brevet of major-general "for gallant and meritorious services at the battles of Winchester and Fisher's Hill, Virginia." His commission was dated October 19th, and he accordingly took rank from that date. But his wound was of such a nature that it was not until near the middle of December that his physical condition permitted his return to active duty. He had had active field service with the artillery as a subaltern and as a chief of an artillery brigade, as well as varied experience with the infantry in command of a regiment, brigade, and division, in many bloody engagements. This service had been wholly with the gallant and well-disciplined Army of the Potomac, in which he had experienced the exhilaration of marked successes, as well as the humiliation of sad disasters. He was now to close his active career as a fighting soldier in the cavalry, and on the 13th of December, although his wound had not yet closed, he reported in person to Major-General Wilson, and was assigned to the command of the Fourth Division of the cavalry corps. His new rank carried with it new responsibilities as well as new honors. It was not without some modest misgivings as to his adaptability to the cavalry service that he turned his back on his comrades in the East to enter upon his new duties in the West. After his assignment, although still physically weak, he proceeded to Memphis, to bring a portion of his command located in that vicinity to the cavalry camp at Gravelly Springs, Alabama.

On his arrival at the cavalry camp he at once entered upon the active work of drill, discipline, and organization. These irksome but vastly important duties received at Upton's hands that thorough attention that characterized all of his labor, for he well knew that the harvest he hoped to reap in the coming campaign would be in direct proportion to the efficient labor which must be expended during the season of preparation. He did this to the complete satisfaction of his corps commander, and he thus so gained the confidence of his own officers and men that both he and they became eagerly anxious for the campaign to open. His hopes and aspirations were at this time thus expressed:

Gravelly Springs, March 14, 1865.

My dear Sister: We expect to break camp tomorrow preparatory to crossing the Tennessee and entering upon the expedition to Alabama. The streams are swollen, which may delay us some days, but it is the intention to move as soon as the weather and roads will permit.

The present campaign, I trust, will seal the doom of the Confederacy. I cannot see how it can be otherwise, unless great and unexpected reverses befall our arms. In that event it will only delay the final result. Peace must soon come, and how welcome it will be to all!

Hobbes was not a soldier, or he never would have advanced the idea that "war is the natural condition of man." I am anxious to be on the move. Camp-life is dull and monotonous, and I always welcome the variety of campaign. Henry's wound worries me considerably, and I fear it will undermine his health. Mine has healed over, but a perverse nerve keeps it constantly in mind. I do not suffer at all from it, only there is a disagreeable sensation about the knee.

Before giving an outline of the campaign, it may be well to devote a few words to the strength and distribution of the enemy's forces available for opposing Wilson's movements, referring briefly in passing to the events that followed the defeat of Hood at Nashville.

After this battle, so disastrous to the enemy, Hood established his headquarters at Tuscumbia, and, early in January, collected the remnants of his infantry at Tupelo, Mississippi. Subsequently, a large part of his force was transferred to the East by the only railroad then open to them from Columbus, Mississippi, Macon,

Augusta, and Columbia, S. C., to enable it to take part in the operations against Sherman in North Carolina. About the latter part of December, General [Nathan Bedford] Forrest, who commanded the enemy's cavalry, collected his corps in the vicinity of Corinth, with the exception of a brigade under Roddy, who was left to cover Hood's rear at Tuscumbia. Another brigade of cavalry under Armstrong was recalled from Corinth to strengthen this force, while Hood's infantry were passing west from Cherokee Station to Tupelo.

It was known to Forrest that he was soon to be placed in command of all the Confederate cavalry which was in the Military Department of Alabama, Mississippi, and East Louisiana, and, therefore, from the time of establishing himself in winter quarters at Corinth, he devoted himself to the concentration, discipline, and reorganization of his command. Bell's and Rucker's brigades of Tennessee cavalry, which were near their homes, and who would with certainty return to their colors, were furloughed for a short time to enable them to procure fresh horses and clothing. The rest of the cavalry was brought to the vicinity of Okolona, Mississippi, a country rich in forage. West Tennessee, Northern Alabama, and Mississippi, beyond the lines of Federal occupation, were thoroughly patrolled to gather in all absentees, and to impress mercilessly all able-bodied men that were fit for service. Picked and trusty scouts were sent into Middle Tennessee to learn all that could be gathered about the contemplated movements of the Union forces.

Forrest assumed his new command in obedience to orders February 24th, and on the 28th received his new rank of lieutenant-general. In reorganizing his corps he had united troops from the same State into brigades and divisions as far as practicable. Thus the Mississippi brigades formed a division commanded by Brigadier-General Chalmers, the Alabama brigades a division under General Buford, and the Tennessee brigades, to which the Texas troops were also added, a division commanded by General Jackson. The famous Second Missouri Cavalry, commanded by Colonel McCulloch, who had heretofore commanded a brigade, were attached to Forrest's headquarters as a special scouting force under Forrest's immediate direction. The aggregate strength of his command at this time was estimated at about ten thousand men.

General Forrest himself was one of the ablest of the Confederate cavalry commanders. He had risen from a subordinate position to the highest honors by merit alone. Although he had had but little education, and no culture, he possessed the native qualities of a leader of cavalry. He was a man of strong will, ready resource, great energy, and untiring activity. These qualifications, united to a sound judgment and quick decision, served to make him a successful commander and a dangerous antagonist. He enforced a pitiless conscription in the territory of his command, and during the period of preparation he devoted himself assiduously to rehorsing his cavalry and artillery, and the complete reorganization of his forces.

By the middle of March, Chalmers's division had an effective aggregate of forty-five hundred men, divided into three brigades, commanded by Brigadier-Generals F. C. Armstrong, Wirt Adams, and P. B. Starke. Jackson's division amounted to thirty-eight hundred men, the two Tennessee brigades of which were commanded by Brigadier-Generals T. H. Bell and A. W. Campbell. Buford was in the vicinity of Montevallo, Alabama, completing the reorganization of his division. Roddy's brigade of this division was located in North Alabama, watching Wilson's movements. The other brigades, Clanton's and Armistead's, were detached to the vicinity of Mobile, guarding its flank approaches.

Forrest had retained his headquarters at Corinth until January 12th; then, leaving Ross's Texans to garrison that place, he removed his headquarters to Verona, Mississippi, fifty-five miles south, where he remained till March 1st, and then established himself at West Point, Mississippi. Wilson's concentration at Gravelly Springs and Waterloo and his preparations for a campaign were early made known to him by Roddy, commanding his advanced brigade. In anticipation of Wilson's movement, Armstrong's and Starke's brigades, thirty-two hundred strong, of Chalmers's division, had been ordered, on the 17th of March, to take post at Pickensville, Alabama; the other brigade, General Wirt Adams, was then moving from Jackson, Mississippi, to Columbus, to protect the line of the

Mobile and Ohio Railroad. Bell's and Campbell's brigades of Jackson's division were concentrated at West Point. The whole of this disposition was due to the uncertainty as to whether Wilson's contemplated campaign had for its object an advance into Mississippi or into Alabama.

It is certain, from what is now known, that great misconception existed on the part of the Confederate commander, Lieutenant-General Richard Taylor, as to the importance and magnitude of General Wilson's design. From his headquarters at Meridian, Mississippi, he informed General Lee, at as late a date as March 27th, that Wilson's movement was a raid, and that it was his intention to meet and whip it before it could advance far into the country. The operations of General Steele's command, which moved from Pensacola on the 20th of March, and was directed on Pollard, threatening Montgomery, had served to distract the enemy, and caused it to appear to be of prime importance. General Buford was therefore directed, March 23d, to move at once from Montevallo to Greenville, via Selma, and Forrest was ordered to send Chalmers's and Jackson's divisions to Selma, with the intention of making a concentration at Greenville to meet this threatening movement of Steele's column. But, before these troops could make much distance southward, they were quickly recalled to meet the more serious danger caused by Wilson's advance. It was now quite patent to the Confederate commander that Wilson's movement would be against Selma, and that it would need all their energy and every available man to interpose in his line of advance to prevent the accomplishment of his object. Forrest, in obedience to telegraphic orders of March 24th, had ordered his forces from the Mississippi line, designing to concentrate them upon Selma before it was definitely known to be Wilson's objective.

General Wilson began his movement south, from Chickasaw and Waterloo, with the First, Second, and Fourth Cavalry Divisions, on the 22d of March. His command numbered twelve thousand five hundred mounted and fifteen hundred dismounted.

They were all veterans, in excellent discipline and condition considering the limited time which had been available for this purpose. But, as they had been assembled in cantonments, freed from the evils of disintegration, and had been thoroughly drilled under the eyes of their own officers, much had been done to make the confidence mutual. The division and other commanders, although mostly young men, were competent and experienced officers, and were full of confidence in themselves and their commands.

Clear and explicit instructions had been given before the march began, and certain discretionary powers had been allowed the division commanders as to march and manoeuvre. The general operations and routes were outlined as far as Selma, and the subsequent movements were to be determined from that point.

Each trooper was directed to carry five days' light rations in haversacks; one pair of extra horseshoes, and one hundred rounds of ammunition. Pack-mules were loaded with five days' rations of hard bread and ten days' sugar and salt. The wagon-train was to carry forty-five days' coffee, twenty days' sugar, fifteen days' salt, and eighty rounds of ammunition. Such was the total allowance for a sixty days' campaign, the allowance of hard bread and forage being limited to that necessary to serve the command while passing through the sterile portions of Alabama. It was expected that it would subsequently live on the country. The supply-train consisted of two hundred and fifty wagons, which were to be sent back as they were emptied, and there was, in addition, a canvas pontoon train of thirty boats, ,transported by fifty-six six-mule teams, under the escort of a battalion of the Twelfth Missouri Cavalry, Major Hubbard commanding.

We will now follow briefly the movements of the cavalry corps, and then direct our attention to the particular operations of the Fourth Division.

Selma, distant about one hundred and eighty miles in a straight line, could only be reached by a fatiguing march of nearly two hundred and fifty. The roads by which the columns moved were at this time very heavy, due to incessant rains, and were intersected by the numerous streams which form the head-waters of the Black Warrior and the Cahawba Rivers. These streams were swollen, their bottom-lands muddy, and the crossings difficult and often dangerous; the country itself is hilly and barren.

The advance was made first on diverging roads: Upton's division moving by the easterly route, through Barton's Station, Russelville, Mount Hope, and Jasper, to Sanders's Ferry, on the West Fork of the Black Warrior River; Long's division by Cherokee Station, Frankfort, Russelville, thence south by the Tuscaloosa road crossing Upper Bear Creek, then turning east by Thorn Hill, crossing the forks of the Buttahatchie, reached Jasper and the ford on the Black Warrior with but little loss of time. McCook's division followed Long's division to Bear Creek, and marched thence toward Tuscaloosa as far as Eldridge, and then eastwardly to Jasper.

Upton's division crossed the Mulberry Fork of the Black Warrior on the 27th. A violent rainstorm filled the streams to their banks, and threatened to prevent the rest of the command from making a junction with it. With great skill and labor this danger was happily averted, and thus an opportunity for a possible partial successful resistance on the part of the enemy was lost, had they known in time of this march and taken advantage of the situation.

From captured scouts of the enemy, Wilson learned at Jasper, on the 27th, that one of Chalmers's brigades (Armstrong's) was marching on Tuscaloosa by Bridgeville. Fearing that Forrest might interpose all of his available forces on his line of advance, he at once decided to strip his divisions to the lightest available marching condition, taking only his pack-train and artillery, and move with the greatest possible rapidity through Elyton to Montevallo. To protect his train, he left with it all of the unmounted troops and a mounted battalion, and directed it to push on as far as Elyton, where it would receive further orders.

The corps moved now with the greatest celerity toward Montevallo, reaching the Cahawba River on the 30th, having marched that day forty-three miles. Thus in nine days Wilson had moved his three divisions over poor roads and through a difficult and sterile country, and had them well in hand for either marching or fighting.

Let us now see what the condition of the enemy was at this time. It will be remembered that Roddy, commanding a brigade of Buford's division, was, until about March 26th, watching Wilson and guarding Northern Alabama; and that through General Taylor's failure to comprehend the true nature or magnitude of the contemplated movement of the cavalry corps, while unduly magnifying Steele's advance from Pensacola, Roddy had been hurried from his very important position and ordered to proceed with all haste to Greenville. General Buford, who was in the vicinity of Montevallo, was ordered to proceed to Greenville March 23d; and Chalmers and Jackson, who had been held in readiness, since March 17th, to march at "six hours' notice," were, on March 25th, ordered to the same point. General Forrest left West Point, Mississippi, March 27th, and at Columbus he learned, through scouts, that Wilson was making for Montevallo, which he immediately reported to his superior officer, General Taylor. He saw at once the threatening character of this movement, and urged the immediate concentration of all possible resources for the defense of Selma.

Forrest, directing Jackson to push forward with the utmost celerity toward Tuscaloosa, reached that point himself on the morning of the 28th, after a ride of thirty hours.

Jackson had started with his command from West Point, Mississippi, on the 26th, and was moving, on the route assigned to him, toward Selma, when he was diverted, as stated above, toward Tuscaloosa. Armstrong's brigade moved from Pickensville March 26th, and was overtaken by General Chalmers with his staff on the 28th, at Greensboro, it having been detained somewhat in the passage of the Black Warrior. At Marion, Armstrong was halted and Starke's brigade ordered thither, in consequence of an order from Forrest prescribing concentration. From the relaxation indulged in by Armstrong's brigade at Marion, and the fact that mere rumors only existed in regard to the movements of the Union forces, it is quite evident that the serious nature of his position had not yet fully penetrated the mind of the enemy. On the afternoon of the 30th Starke's brigade reached Marion, and that night at eleven o'clock orders were received from General Taylor, directing the division to move upon Plantersville. Hence at this epoch, March 30th, we find Forrest's command scattered in every direction, and without any apparent directing head or plan of operations.

Meanwhile Wilson, at Elyton, had dispatched Croxton's brigade, of McCook's division, fifteen hundred strong, on the 30th, to attempt the capture of Tuscaloosa, and, if successful, to destroy the stores and rejoin the main column, via Centreville. If, however, he found the enemy in force, he was to hold them in check and prevent a junction with the rest of Forrest's command in Wilson's immediate front. On his way to Tuscaloosa he fell in with the rearguard of Jackson's division at Trion, and interposed himself between it and Jackson's trains.

This occurred on the 31st, and Jackson, who had reached within eight miles of Scottsboro, on his way from Tuscaloosa to join Forrest, determined to attack him early the next morning. This he did, capturing some prisoners, but not crippling Croxton in the least, who immediately moved northeasterly by an unfrequented road, and marched rapidly for ten or fifteen miles, then turned west, and, after a forty-mile march that day, arrived at Johnson's Ferry on the Black Warrior River. General Jack-son, somewhat elated at his success, sent a dispatch to the commanding officer at Tuscaloosa, informing him that he had dispersed Croxton's force, and added: "It is scattered in the mountains and cannot again be collected. Assure the fair ladies that the tread of the vandal hordes shall not pollute the streets of their beautiful city." As a sequel to this, it may here be stated that Croxton marched thirty-two miles the next day, and at 10 p. m. arrived on the opposite side of the river from Tuscaloosa, and received the surrender of the town at 1 a. m. on the 3d.

When Wilson heard, through dispatches captured at Randolph, that Jackson was being delayed by Croxton, he immediately sent McCook with La Grange's brigade to Centreville, where the road from Trion crosses the Cahawba, to make a junction with Croxton, or at least hold Jackson in check and prevent his joining Forrest. McCook met Jackson on April 2d, and, finding him too strong, burned the bridge over the Cahawba at Centreville, thus preventing Jackson's crossing the Cahawba, and effectually eliminating

Jackson's division from all participation in opposing his march to Selma. McCook, after accomplishing this important service, marched via Randolph, joined the trains on the 5th of April, and brought them safely into Selma.

Let us next ascertain what became of Chalmers's two brigades. Moving at 11 p. m., on the 30th, from Marion to Plantersville, owing to bad roads and delay about pontoon train, Chalmers, with Starke's brigade, did not cross the Cahawba till late on the 31st. Then swamps and the condition of the roads caused him to diverge from his projected route, and seek a more practicable way, encumbered as he was with the artillery and trains of the command. Forrest, not knowing where he was, in the meantime telegraphed Taylor at Selma for information, and received in reply an answer to the effect that he was at Plantersville, which at that time was in the rear of Forrest's advanced position at Randolph. Under the impression that this information was correct, Forrest claims that he ordered the position at Ebenezer Church to be held, making allowance for this brigade in the disposition of his troops. Armstrong's brigade having been detached from his command on April 1st, joined Forrest at 11 p. m. of that day, on the road between Marion and Plantersville.

Roddy, having crossed the Alabama at Selma on his way south to Greenville, was directed to turn about on March 30th, and hasten north to report to General Daniel Adams at Montevallo. Recrossing the river and making a forced march of fifty miles, he reached Montevallo in time to participate in the defense of that field.

The generalship on the part of the Confederates had succeeded in throwing out of Wilson's path three of their best brigades, viz., Bell's and Campbell's of Jackson's division, and Starke's of Chalmers's division, together with the artillery of Forrest's corps, and leaving only Armstrong's, Roddy's, and Crossland's brigades, and the inferior troops which Adams had collected together in the vicinity of Montevallo, to oppose him. We can now follow understandingly the active operations of the Federal cavalry.

Upton's division, leading, reached Montevallo on the evening of March 30th, having destroyed important and valuable iron-works during the day. He was ordered to await the arrival of the corps, and

111

before noon of the next day the command was again concentrated. At Montevallo the first serious stand was made by the enemy, whose forces consisted of Roddy's brigade, coming up after a forced march from Selma, Crossland's Kentucky brigade, and other troops collected by General Daniel Adams, who commanded the whole.

From the belfry of the village church, Upton's line of mounted skirmishers could be seen a mile in front of the village, and occasional puffs of smoke told that the enemy was feeling our lines. Upton's troopers, not on the skirmish-line, were massed behind the village in some fields, out of view of the enemy, while Long's splendid division of five thousand troopers was slowly closing up. Upton had ordered his skirmishers to retire slowly before the enemy, and toward 1 p. m. his men could be seen moving in skirmishing order toward the Union lines. Moving to the rear and wheeling about to fire, every movement was marked with cool precision. When he had retired within a few hundred yards of the village the corps commander said: "Upton, I think you have let them come far enough; move out!" In a moment the skirmish-line was re-enforced, and Upton moved down the road with his main body in column of fours at the trot until clear of the village, when the Fifth Iowa, Colonel Young commanding, made a handsome charge, driving the enemy and capturing fifty prisoners from Roddy's command and Crossland's Kentucky Brigade. The enemy disputed every creek-bottom and ridge with great stubbornness, but Upton's impetuosity, ably seconded by that of his brigade commanders, Winslow and Alexander, drove everything before him. When the enemy had been forced back to Six-Mile Creek, the command halted for the night on the road to Randolph, and on the next day at dawn entered that place.

At Randolph, Upton's scouts captured the important dispatches from Jackson to Forrest, and from Forrest to Jackson, before referred to, which gave Wilson the key to the whole situation. From the first he learned that Forrest, with a part of his command, was in his front, a fact he had already obtained from prisoners captured; that Jackson, with his division, and all the wagons and artillery of the Confederate cavalry, marching from Tuscaloosa via Trion toward Centreville, had encamped the night before at Hill's plantation, three miles beyond Scottsboro; that Croxton, with the brigade detached at Elyton, had struck Jackson's rear-guard at Trion, and interposed himself between it and the train; that Jackson had discovered this, and intended to attack Croxton at daylight, April 1st. He learned from the other dispatch that Chalmers had also arrived at Marion, Alabama, and had been ordered to cross to the east side of the Cahawba, for the purpose of joining Forrest in front, or in the works at Selma. Also that a force of dismounted men were stationed at Centreville, with orders to hold the bridge over the Cahawba as long as possible, and in no event to let it fall into the hands of the Federals.

Shortly after the interception of these dispatches, Wilson heard from Croxton at Trion, the night before, that he had struck Jackson's rear; and, instead of pushing on toward Tuscaloosa, as he was ordered, he would follow and endeavor to bring him to an engagement, hoping thereby to prevent his junction with Forrest.

Having this information, Wilson directed McCook to strengthen the battalion previously ordered to Centreville by a regiment, and to follow with LaGrange's entire brigade, leaving all pack-trains and wagons with the main column, so that he could march with the utmost celerity; and, after seizing the Centreville bridge and leaving it under the protection of a sufficient guard, to cross the Cahawba, and continue his march by the Scottsboro road toward Trion. His orders were to attack and break up Jackson's forces, form a junction with Croxton if practicable, and rejoin the corps with his entire division by the Centreville road to Selma. Although McCook did not leave Randolph till near 11 a. m., and the distance to Scottsboro-was nearly forty miles, Wilson hoped by the movement to do more than secure the Centreville bridge, and prevent Jackson from joining the force in front of the main column.

On the next morning the march was resumed, Upton taking the left-hand or eastern road, and Long confronting the enemy. Long skirmished all day, driving the enemy slowly but steadily before him.

At 3 p. m., Forrest, having been re-enforced by Armstrong's brigade, and some militia, halted near Ebenezer Church, five miles from Plantersville, and gave battle. Forrest chose his position north of Bogler's Creek, his right resting on Mulberry Creek, his left on a high wooded ridge. He posted three pieces of artillery on the Randolph road and two on the Maplesville road, upon which Upton was advancing. His forces consisted of Roddy's brigade, Crossland's Kentucky brigade, Armstrong's brigade, and three hundred infantry just from Selma.

As soon as Long could deploy, he made his attack, and Upton, always prompt and fortunate, hearing the cheers and firing, took the trot and turned the right flank of the enemy at the opportune moment.

Forrest, expecting to be re-enforced by Chalmers, who was reported within supporting distance, but who had really gone to Marion with Starke's brigade, placed his line of battle in front of the forks of the roads, with three guns on the left-hand road, on which Long was advancing. The right-hand road was not well watched or strongly held, as Upton's advance met with but little resistance. A squadron of the Seventeenth Indiana, Miller's brigade, Long's division, charged the three-gun battery with sabers, crushed down the gun-carriages, and passed beyond, but were driven back by the enemy's supports. The sharp fighting soon resulted in forcing Forrest in confusion from the field with a loss of three guns and four hundred prisoners. That night the two Union divisions camped at Plantersville, nineteen miles from Selma. At this place the enemy, having halted to obtain forage and subsistence stores, were driven out in hot haste, Forrest, with his escort, making a gallant resistance.

At daylight of the 2d of April our troops moved out on the Summerville road, Long's division leading, closely followed by Upton. The enemy offered no resistance, and early in the afternoon the advanced troopers came in sight of Selma. At Elyton, Upton had obtained and sent to corps headquarters detailed information of the defenses, of the general correctness of which Wilson satisfied himself afterward by a careful reconnaissance.

Selma is situated on the north bank of the Alabama River, about one hundred feet above the mean level of the water. It contained an arsenal and foundries for making shot and shell, and was the most important depot of the enemy in the Southwest.

Its fortifications consisted of a continuous line of infantry parapets, with ample works for artillery defense, surrounding the city at a distance of three miles, with its flanks resting on the Alabama River. An interior line of stronger profile was also partially constructed. These works were defended by a force nearly seven thousand strong, consisting of Roddy's, Armstrong's, and Crossland's brigades of cavalry, and the militia and infantry collected by General Daniel Adams, all under the command of Forrest himself. So rapid had been the advance of the national cavalry that the town was invested before Chalmers, with Starke's brigade, could reach it from Marion.

Wilson had his troops in position shortly after 4 p. m. He directed Long to march by the flanks of brigades, approach the city, and cross to the Summerville road, without exposing his men, and to develop his line as soon as he could arrive in front of the works. Upton was directed to move on the Range Line road, sending a squadron on the Burnsville road.

Having decided to assault the works without delay, Long was directed to move diagonally across the road upon which his troops were posted, while Upton, at his own request, with a picked force of three hundred men, was directed to penetrate the swamps upon his left, break through the line covered by it, and turn the enemy's right, the rest of his division to conform to the movement. The signal for the advance was to be the discharge of a single gun from Rodney's battery, to be given as soon as Upton's turning movement had developed itself.

Before that plan could be executed, and while waiting for the signal to advance, Long was informed that a strong force of the Confederate cavalry had begun skirmishing with his rear, and threatened a general attack upon his pack-train and led horses. He had left a force of six companies well posted at the creek in anticipation of that movement, afterward ascertained to have been made by Chalmers in obedience to the instructions of Forrest. Fearing lest the affair might compromise the assault upon the main position, Long (having strengthened the rear by another regiment) determined to make the assault without waiting for the signal, and gave the order to advance. His command was formed in single line, dismounted, the Seventeenth Indiana Mounted Infantry on the right, and next, from right to left, the One Hundred and Twenty-third Illinois Mounted Infantry, Ninety-eighth Illinois Mounted Infantry, Fourth Ohio Cavalry, and Fourth Michigan Cavalry; in all eleven hundred and sixty officers and men. They had to charge across open ground six hundred yards to the works, exposed to the fire of artillery and musketry, and that part of the line which they were to assault was manned by Armstrong's brigade, numbering fifteen hundred men, and regarded as the best of Forrest's corps. Long's dismounted troops, all armed with the Spencer magazine gun, sprang forward in an unfaltering manner. The flanks had some difficulty in crossing a ravine and marshy soil, but in less than fifteen minutes the line had swept over the works and driven the Confederates in confusion toward the city. But the loss was considerable, being in all forty killed and two hundred and sixty wounded, and among the wounded was General Long himself, who was temporarily succeeded in command by Colonel Minty. Wilson, arriving on that part of the field just after the works were carried, at once notified Upton of Long's success, and directed Colonel Minty to form Long's division for a new advance. The garrison had occupied the new line near the edge of the city. A gallant charge by the Fourth United States Cavalry was repulsed, but it rapidly reformed on the left. It was now quite dark. Upton's division advancing at the same time, a new charge was made by the Fourth Ohio, Seventeenth Indiana, and Fourth United States Cavalry, dismounted. The troops, inspired by the wildest enthusiasm, swept everything before them, and penetrated the city in all directions. Upton's division, though encountering less resistance, charged with its habitual spirit and devotion. It is said that the men, finding it too difficult to break down or pry away the sharp-pointed stockade in front of the earthworks, those behind, coming on swiftly, jumped on the shoulders of the foremost and leaped the obstructions, thus storming the works by a game of "leap-frog."

The garrison fought with great coolness and skill. Forrest was reported to have been engaged personally in two or three romantic combats, and he, with Generals Armstrong, Roddy, Adams, and a number of men, escaped under cover of darkness by the Burnsville or river road. A portion of Upton's division pursued on the Burnsville road until long after midnight, capturing four guns and many prisoners. The immediate fruit of the victory was thirty-one field guns and one thirty-pound Parrott, twenty-seven hundred prisoners, including one hundred and fifty officers, a number of colors, three thousand horses, and a large quantity of stores of every kind.

As soon as the troops could be assembled and got into camp, General Winslow was assigned to the command of the city, with orders to destroy everything that could benefit the Confederate cause.

In the excitement of the hour some acts of plunder and vandalism were perhaps committed, but order was soon restored by an active provost guard.

General Upton was directed to march at daylight the next morning with his division for the purpose of driving Chalmers west of the Cahawba, to open communication with McCook, who was expected from Centreville, and to assist him in bringing in the train. On the 5th, McCook and Upton arrived with the train, but nothing definite had been heard of Croxton.

On April 6th, Wilson, having ordered his engineer officer to lay the bridge, which had been preparing, over the Alabama River, with the utmost dispatch, went to Cahawba to see Forrest, who had agreed to meet him there under a flag of truce to arrange an exchange of prisoners. Wilson soon discovered that he need not expect liberality in the matter, and that Forrest hoped to recapture the prisoners in his hands. During the conversation Wilson learned from Forrest that Croxton had had an engagement with Wirt Adams near Bridgeville, forty miles southwest of Tuscaloosa, two days before.

This assured Wilson of Croxton's success and safety, and he determined to lose no time in crossing to the south side of the Alabama. Returning to Selma, he urged everyone to the utmost exertions. The river was quite full and rising, its current swift, strong, and full of floating drift-wood. The weather was also unsettled and rainy, but by great labor night and day the bridge, eight hundred and seventy feet long, was completed. During the night it was lighted by the blaze of burning buildings, and the command had all crossed by daylight of the 10th. Behind them, in the destroyed arsenal, foundries, arms, stores, and military munitions of every kind, the national troops had left immense ruin. They had struck the Confederacy a disastrous blow.

In determining his future course from Selma, Wilson had carefully considered all the influencing circumstances. He consulted Upton freely and fully, and had his concurrence and approval in the plan of operations adopted. Generals Grant and Thomas had given him discretionary powers and a roving commission. Two routes lay open before him: one, to proceed to Mobile and assist Canby; the other, to march east and unite his forces with those of Sherman. He chose the latter, for he rightly conjectured that Mobile itself would soon fall, almost before he could reach that place, and he could be of no particular advantage to Canby. The great supply depot for the use of the besieged having been destroyed, and the heart of the State being in his possession, the fall of Mobile was a question of a few days at the farthest, for he knew from the Confederate papers of the close investment of the defenses, and his cavalry command would scarcely be of any more advantage to Canby than the division already there. Subsequent results confirmed the wisdom of his decision, for Spanish Fort was evacuated on April 8th, Blakely was carried by assault on the 9th, and Mobile fell on the 13th.

He therefore put his corps in motion for Montgomery, with LaGrange's brigade, of McCook's division, in the advance. Skirmishing with some Alabama cavalry, the next day's march brought the command to the beautiful town of Lownesboro. The next day McCook's division entered Montgomery without resistance, and the troops were gladdened with the sight of the United States flag flying from the dome of the Capitol, where the Confederate flag had been raised four years before.

The remainder of the campaign is given with sufficient detail for our purpose in Upton's report of the operations of his division, which is here inserted in full as a typical document, showing personal modesty, unstinted liberality to his associate and subordinate commanders, and praise to his worthy troopers.

Headquarters Fourth Division Cavalry Corps, Military Division of the Mississippi, May, 1865.

Major E. B. Beaumont, Assistant Adjutant-General,

Cavalry Corps, M. D. M.

I have the honor to submit the following report of the operations of the Fourth Cavalry Division during the late campaign:

To avoid delay in leaving Chickasaw, the train was sent on the 19th of March to Cherokee Station, on the Memphis and Charleston Railroad, and was followed by the First Brigade, commanded by brevet Brigadier-General Winslow on the 21st.

The general movement commenced on the 22d of March; Winslow's brigade and train camping near Throckmorton's Mill; the Second Brigade, commanded by brevet Brigadier-General Alexander, camping on Cave Creek, twenty-five miles from Chickasaw.

March 23d.—Left Russellville to our right, and camped at Newbury, distance thirty miles. Found plenty of corn and provisions.

March 24th.—March resumed, General Alexander moving from Mount Hope via Houston toward Clear Creek Falls, General Winslow and train via Kinlock, and Hubbard's Mill on head-waters of Sipsey. The road was exceedingly mountainous, and forage scarce. First Brigade made sixteen miles.

March 25th.—Brigades united and camped at Clear Creek Falls, distance thirty miles. Country almost destitute of forage.

March 26th.—Winslow was directed to move via Bartonville and Hanly's Mill toward Elyton; Alexander and train via Jasper and Democrat. Winslow, finding the Sipsey River unfordable, moved down the Black Warrior to Sanders's Ferry, where the division camped for

119

the night—distance twenty-three miles; forage found below Sanders's Ferry.

March 27th.—Crossed Black Warrior over an extremely dangerous ford. Alexander's brigade camped on the east bank of Locust Ford. Winslow's brigade marched all night and arrived on west bank at 4 a. m. next day; distance fifteen miles. Provisions and forage scarce.

March 28th.—Marched at 10 a. m.; Alexander's brigade camping at Elyton, Winslow's on Hawkins's plantation, two miles west; distance twenty miles. The road was exceedingly rough. At the end of the day's march we debouched into a beautiful valley, rich in provisions and forage.

Patterson's regiment from Northern Alabama passed through Elyton, just before the arrival of the division, its rear-guard being driven out by General Alexander's advance.

By direction of the brevet major-general commanding the corps, the train remained at Elyton till the arrival of the corps train.

March 29th.—The division moved at 10.30 a. m., with a view to secure a crossing over the Cahawba River that night; but the ford having been obstructed by Patterson's regiment, and a heavy rain setting in, which soon raised the river, prevented more than one regiment getting across; distance fifteen miles. The McIlvaine and Rich Mountain Iron-Works were destroyed near Elyton.

March 30th.—General Winslow converted the railroad-bridge over the Cahawba into a foot-bridge, and at 9.30 a. m. the crossing commenced. The division camped at Montevallo; distance, seventeen miles. Roads were bad; forage and provisions found in abundance around Montevallo. A colliery and the Central Iron-Works were destroyed near the Cahawba, while detachments sent out from Montevallo destroyed the Columbiana and Bibb Iron-Works.

There being strong indications of the enemy's presence in large force, the division awaited the arrival of the corps.

March 31st.—The brevet major-general commanding the corps having arrived, I was directed to move out at 1.30 p. m. About two miles south of the town the advance of Roddy's division was encountered. It was immediately charged by General Alexander, and driven back in great confusion upon their main position beyond a difficult creek, abandoning arms and accoutrements at every step.

Dispositions were at once made to turn the enemy's right, while Rodney's Battery I, Fourth United States Artillery, was placed in position and opened fire. After some skirmishing, without awaiting a trial of arms, the enemy withdrew.

General Winslow now took up the pursuit, and by a series of brilliant and impetuous charges drove the enemy until late in the night, capturing many prisoners, arms, and accoutrements. The division, elated with having ridden down the enemy in every conflict during the day, camped three miles north of Randolph, having made fourteen miles.

April 1st.—The pursuit was resumed as far as Randolph, where, pursuant to your instructions, the division took the road to the left, leading to Old Maplesville, leaving the main Selma road, along which the enemy retired, for General Long's division. To cover the movement, the advance-guard was directed to pursue the enemy a mile and a half, and then remain till relieved by General Long's division. Proceeding about four miles to the left of Randolph, my command took a road to the right, leading through Maplesville Station, and intersecting the main Selma road at Ebenezer Church.

Anticipating an opportunity to flank the enemy at this point, the march of the division was hastened, and at 4 p. m. he was found in position, his force, commanded by General Forrest in person, consisting of infantry, artillery, and cavalry, his right resting on Mulberry Creek, and his left on a high wooded ridge near Bogler's Creek. General Alexander threw his brigade into action, dismounted with great celerity, and, after a stubborn fight of an hour's duration, routed the enemy and captured his guns. General Winslow took up the pursuit with his brigade mounted, captured three hundred prisoners and drove the enemy through Plantersville, nineteen miles from Selma, when the division camped for the night, having made twenty miles.

April 2d.—The division marched at 10 a. m. for Selma, following the Second Division, arriving in front of the fortifications on the Plantersville road at 4 p. m. It was being placed in position, preparatory to a night attack on the enemy's right, when Long's division carried the work in its front. The division was immediately ordered forward, the skirmish-line driving the enemy from the works in its front, and capturing five pieces of artillery. General Winslow brought forward the Fourth Iowa at a gallop, and, charging into the city in various directions, captured several pieces of artillery and several hundred prisoners. The Seventh Ohio Cavalry was sent out on the Burnsville road, and captured four guns, one hundred and twenty-five prisoners, and many small-arms.

April 3d.—The division moved out from Selma with instructions to pursue the remnants of Forrest's command across the Cahawba River, and to meet and escort the general train to the city. It returned on the 6th, having made a circuit of ninety miles.

April 8th.—At 9 p. m. the division commenced crossing the Alabama River on a pontoon-bridge. The passage was soon interrupted by the descent of drift-wood, which carried the bridge away. The bridge was repaired at about 2 p. m. on the 9th, and the crossing was resumed, but was again interrupted by descending drift-wood. The breach was repaired by 6 p. m., and at 9 p. m. the division was across and encamped on the south bank. General Alexander narrowly escaped with his life while endeavoring to pass a heavy log safely under the bridge.

April 10th.—Marched for Montgomery, and encamped at Church Hill; distance, twenty-four miles. Plenty of forage.

April nth.—Marched at 5.30 a. m.; crossed Big Swamp or Big Swamp Creek, and camped at Colonel Harrison's, four miles east of Lownesboro; distance, twelve miles.

April 12th.—Marched at 5.30 a. m.; passed through Montgomery at 4 o'clock p. m., and camped four miles east on Columbus road; distance, twenty-seven miles.

LaGrange's brigade, of McCook's division, having been placed under my command, I received orders on the 14th to march to the Chattahoochee to secure the bridge over that river, either at Columbus or West Point, thereby opening for the cavalry corps the road into Georgia. In pursuance of these instructions, I sent LaGrange's brigade, via Tuskegee and Opelika, to West Point, where he arrived on the 16th. He immediately attacked the garrison at that place, capturing it and securing the bridge. My own division marched directly on Columbus, eighty miles distant.

Columbus is a fortified city of twelve thousand inhabitants, situated on the east bank of the Chattahoochee. Three bridges span the river at this point: one a foot-bridge at the lower end of the city; the others, a foot and a railroad bridge, are three-fourths of a mile above, opposite the upper end of the city. There is a fourth bridge at Clapp's Factory, three miles above, which was destroyed upon the approach of Captain Young, of the Tenth Missouri, who was sent to secure it.

On the west bank of the river, between the upper and lower bridges, lies the small town of Girard. Mill Creek, which flows through an open valley about a mile in width, separating two prominent ridges, which approach the river perpendicularly, and overlook the city, empties into the river near the center of Girard. The lower bridge was defended from the east bank by a rifle-pit, with three pieces of artillery sweeping it. The upper foot and railroad bridges were defended by a *tete-de-pont* consisting of two redoubts connected by a range of rifle-pits about three quarters of a mile in length, extending across the upper ridge, well strengthened by felled timber in front. The lower redoubt, situated just below the upper ridge, contained six and twelve pounder howitzers. Four and ten pounder Parrott guns were in position on its right. These guns completely swept Mill Creek Valley. The upper redoubt contained four guns commanding the Summerfield road.

Five guns swept the railroad and two eight-inch howitzers the upper foot-bridge, making in all twenty-four guns in position.

The works were held by about twenty-seven hundred infantry. The division, moving along the lower Crawford road, arrived opposite the lower bridge at about 2 p. m. Colonel Eggleston, commanding the advance-guard, immediately charged to secure it, but was received with a heavy fire of artillery and musketry, while the bridge, previously prepared with combustible material, was at the same time fired. He therefore retired behind the ridge. Rodney's battery fired a few shots, which developed the position of the enemy's artillery.

It being impossible to attack the *tete-de-pont* from this direction, Alexander's brigade was placed in position along the crest of the lower ridge, while Winslows brigade, making a wide detour, was sent, under cover, across to the Summerfield road on the upper ridge.

His brigade was preceded by two companies of the Fifth Iowa Cavalry, under Captain Lewis, who drove in the opposing picket and charged gallantly upon a strong line of works which, in the darkness, appeared to be the enemy's main position. General Winslow at once disposed his command for the attack, the plan of which was, to penetrate the works with dismounted men, and then to send a mounted force through the breach, with directions to charge directly upon the bridge.

The assault was made about 9 p. m., under cover of darkness, by six companies of the Third Iowa Cavalry, commanded by Colonel Noble. The first line of works was soon carried, and, being mistaken for the main line, two companies of the Tenth Missouri were ordered to charge the bridge. These companies, supposed by the enemy to be their own men, passed through the works on the Summerfield road unharmed, charged and secured the bridge, capturing many prisoners. Captain McGlasson, finding himself in the enemy's rear and vastly outnumbered, rejoined his regiment.

In the meantime the main line opened fire upon the right with grape and musketry. The Third Iowa pressed forward through a slashing a hundred yards deep, and, after a charge unexampled in cavalry service, and with but few parallels in infantry, crowned the works.

General Winslow promptly followed up the success. Ignoring the redoubt on the right, which still continued its fire, the Fourth Iowa, dismounted, under Captain Abraham, passed through the breach, turned to the right, charged the redoubt, captured ten guns, and then, sweeping across the bridge with the flying rebels, captured two howitzers, loaded with grape and canister, at the opposite end.

Mounted companies from the same regiment followed in rear of Captain Abraham, and, after crossing the bridge, turned to the right and charged in flank the works at the lower bridge, capturing prisoners and the three guns at that point.

By 10 p. m., Columbus, with its vast munitions of war, fifteen hundred prisoners, and twenty-four guns, was in our hands. This victory, which was the closing conflict of the war, was achieved with the loss of but thirty men killed and wounded.

April 18th, at 8.30 a. m., the division marched for Macon, via Double Bridge and Thomaston, arriving and going into camp at East Macon on the evening of the 21st. The march was through a rich country, and the distance was ninety-eight miles. Here, official information of the armistice between Generals Sherman and Johnston having been received, the campaign closed.

The conduct of the officers and men during the campaign is deserving of the highest commendation. Whether mounted or dismounted, but one spirit prevailed, and that was to run over the enemy wherever found or whatever might be his numbers. Nothing but the impetuosity of the charges, whereby the enemy was not given time to defend himself, can account for the small list of casualties, amounting in all to ninety-eight killed and wounded. In every conflict the troops actually engaged were vastly outnumbered.

At Ebenezer Church, General Alexander routed Forrest's command with less than one thousand men, while General Winslow carried the formidable works at Columbus with but eleven hundred men. From the members of my staff—Brevet-Major James W. Latta, Assistant Adjutant-General; Captain Tom C. Gilpin, acting Aide-de-camp; Lieutenant Sloan Keck, acting Aide-de-camp; Lieutenant Peter Keck, Ordnance Officer—I received, on all occasions, prompt and gallant assistance.

The division arrived at Macon in good fighting condition.

I respectfully refer you to the accompanying reports of the brigade commanders, in which the charges of the regiments under their commands are minutely described, also mentioning the names of officers and men distinguishing themselves for gallantry and soldierly conduct.

In conclusion, I desire to ascribe the success of the division, in the first degree to the zeal, energy, 8 and ability displayed by Generals Winslow and Alexander, commanding First and Second Brigades. They have shown in every battle great skill and gallantry, and possess, in an eminent degree, all the qualities of cavalry officers. I respectfully urge their immediate promotion for the good of the service. Inclosed is a list of officers and men who have distinguished themselves and are entitled to promotion.

Very respectfully, your obedient servant,

E. Upton,

Brevet Major-General Commanding Fourth Division.

In the brief campaign which we have described, Upton's success as a cavalry officer had been so conspicuous that it satisfied not only his corps commander but himself. In his enthusiasm over the capture of Columbus, under cover of darkness, he frequently remarked that he had just learned one of the greatest possibilities of war, and did not doubt that he could go anywhere in the Confederacy, and do anything which might be required of his division. It gave him a practical lesson in regard to the relative proportions and power of the three arms in the make-up of an army, which he could never have had without the experience of this campaign.

A brief reference to Croxton's operations will serve to complete the story of this campaign.

Croxton's brigade, of McCook's division, consisted of the Second Michigan Cavalry, the Fourth Kentucky Mounted Infantry, the Sixth Kentucky Cavalry, and the Eighth Iowa Cavalry, fifteen hundred effective in all. He took no artillery nor train, save one headquarters baggage-wagon, three ambulances, and the allowance of pack-mules. Each trooper had one hundred and twenty rounds of ammunition, and was armed with the Spencer carbine. After the capture of Tuscaloosa, knowing that Jack-son and Chalmers were between him and Selma, he thought it too hazardous to reach that place via Centreville. He therefore decided to move toward Eutaw, in the hope of crossing the Black Warrior lower down, and cutting the railroad between Selma and Demopolis.

On the 5th of April he recrossed the Black Warrior, burned the bridge, marched out on the Columbus (Mississippi) road, and on the 6th turned toward Eutaw. The same morning General Wirt Adams, with fifteen hundred men, left Pickensville at seven o'clock, intending to join Forrest via Finche's Ferry. Croxton at that time thought his force was larger.

About 2 p. m. Adams's men began to annoy the rear of Croxton's brigade, near Pleasant Ridge. Meantime Croxton had recrossed the Sipsey River and turned on the military road toward Tuscaloosa. About 5 p. m. Adams charged the rear of Croxton with much vigor, and captured or disabled about a third of the Sixth Kentucky Cavalry. The Second Michigan formed line, and, by a series of successful volleys, succeeded in saving the rest of the Kentucky regiment, and completely held the advancing enemy in check, and caused, at dark, their withdrawal with considerable loss. After accomplishing this, this gallant regiment marched on and overtook the rest of the brigade in camp at twelve o'clock.

On the 7th, Croxton went into camp at North-port, a few miles from Tuscaloosa. His foraging parties and scouts on the road to Columbus misled Adams, who, believing Columbus to be Croxton's objective, turned his column in that direction and arrived there at 1 p. m. on the 8th, having marched forty-five miles in eleven hours. This put him seventy miles northwest of Croxton. Chalmers was moving toward Columbus at the same time, and arrived there on the 9th.

On the 12th, Croxton, having successfully accomplished the purpose of his diversion, marched northward, and, passing on through Jasper, recrossed the West Fork of the Black Warrior at Hanly's Mills, marched nearly due east via Mount Penson and Trussville, crossed the Coosa at True's and Collins's Ferries, and continued on to Talladega, a region rich in mineral resources. On the 22d of April, the Eighth Iowa being in advance, he charged into Talladega, putting General B. H. Hill's brigade to flight. Replenishing haversacks, he pushed on northeastwardly on the 23d, destroying the railroad and skirmishing with Hill, who was falling back to Jacksonville. In the region of the Blue Mountains, Croxton destroyed valuable iron and niter works, besides railroad-bridges, depots, and rolling-stock.

On the 25th, Croxton moved out on the road leading to Newham, Georgia. The next day, while crossing the Chattahoochee, he heard of the fall of Richmond, the surrender of Lee, and the assassination of Lincoln. He arrived, with his brigade in good condition, at Forsyth, Georgia, April 29th, and reported to General Wilson, then at Macon, Georgia. Without delay the cavalry corps was distributed throughout Georgia and Florida to receive the surrender of detached commands, and within a few weeks most of the regiments were mustered out of the service.

Upton was sent to Augusta, Georgia, and took possession of the United States Arsenal and other public property there. On this occasion, as he raised the United States flag on the arsenal-grounds (May 8, 1865), he thus addressed his command:

"Soldiers! Four years ago the Governor of Georgia, at the head of an armed force, hauled down the American flag at this arsenal. The

President of the United States called the nation to arms to repossess the forts and arsenals which had been seized. After four years of sanguinary war and conflict we execute the order of the great preserver of union and liberty, and today we again hoist the stars and stripes over the United States Arsenal at Augusta. Majestically, triumphantly she rises!"

But Peace, with her manifold blessings, had come. Our gallant soldiers had done their part to save the country from destruction. The claims of home and family now began to assert themselves with renewed strength as the days of battle receded. And how grandly our volunteer soldiers at once put off the "pomp and circumstance of glorious war," to begin again the patient toil for their daily bread, history records to their undying honor and glory.

The parting of the troops from their trusted commanders shows depth of feeling and devotion possible only among men who love liberty and fight to maintain it. As a type of this heart-felt affection which bound them together we have this testimonial.

Atlanta, May 24, 1865.

Brevet Major-General E. Upton,

Commanding Fourth Division Cavalry Corps, Military Division of the Mississippi.

General: In behalf of the officers and men it has been my high honor to command, I hereby tender to you the regrets of the Tenth Regiment of Cavalry, Missouri Volunteers, at the sundering of the ties that have bound us together during the past five months.

Believe me, general, that the pleasure of laying down our arms and resuming the peaceful avocations of citizens, and the bright prospect of a happy peace for our beloved country, alone take away any of the pangs caused by this separation. The march from Chickasaw to Macon, embracing the glorious fields of "Montevallo," "Ebenezer Church," "Selma," and "Columbus," has proved to us the kindness of your heart toward your comrades in arms, and the fact that you are justly entitled to the honors your country has conferred upon you.

Under you my regiment has terminated a glorious term of service by a campaign unsurpassed by any during the wars of modern times.

The memory of that campaign shall ever remain fresh and bright in all our hearts.

In conclusion, receive from us a farewell the bitter of which is sweetened by our bright prospects for the future.

With much esteem I remain your obedient servant,

F. W. Benteen, Lieutenant-Colonel, Commanding Tenth Cavalry,
Missouri Volunteers.

Captain (brevet lieutenant-colonel) Frederick William Benteen (1834–1898) is most famous for having provided excellent leadership to the survivors of the Little Bighorn disaster in 1876. He was the recipient of General Custer's final note on June 25th, 1876, telling Benteen to quickly bring up the pack-train with ammunition. By the time Benteen arrived in the position of Major Marcus Reno, who had engaged the Sioux and Cheyenne warriors and been repulsed, Custer was miles downstream fighting overwhelming numbers of warriors. Shortly afterwards, the warriors converged on Reno and Benteen and forced them back into a shallow swale, known today as the Reno-Benteen defense area. The soldiers were under siege there until dark and all the next day. The Native Americans left the Little Bighorn Valley on the evening of the 26th, knowing that Generals Alfred Terry and John Gibbon were approaching from the west. At the Reno Court of Inquiry in 1879, one soldier said of Benteen, "His conduct for coolness and gallantry was perfectly superb, no other word would express it."—Ed. 2016

This sentiment of affection was mutual between Upton and his command, and on taking leave of his soldiers he issued this order:

Headquarters Fourth Division Cavalry Corps, Military Division of
the Mississippi,

Edgefield, Tenn., June 10, 1865.

General Orders No. 21.

Before severing his connection with the command, the brevet major-general commanding desires to express his high appreciation of the bravery, endurance, and soldierly qualities displayed by the officers and men of his division in the late cavalry campaign. Leaving Chickasaw, Alabama, on the 22d of March as a new organization and without status in the cavalry corps, you in one month traversed six hundred miles, crossed six rivers, met and defeated the enemy at Montevallo, Alabama, capturing one hundred prisoners; routed

Forrest, Buford, and Roddy in their chosen position at Ebenezer Church, capturing two guns and three hundred prisoners; carried the works in your front at Selma, capturing thirteen guns, eleven hundred prisoners, and five battle-flags; and finally crowned your successes by a night assault upon the enemy's intrenchments at Columbus, Georgia, where you captured fifteen hundred prisoners, twenty-four guns, eight battle-flags, and vast munitions of war.

April 21st, you arrived at Macon, Georgia, having captured on your march three thousand prisoners, thirty-nine pieces of artillery, and thirteen battle-flags.

Whether mounted, with the saber, or dismounted, with the carbine, the brave men of the Third, Fourth, and Fifth Iowa, First and Seventh Ohio, and Tenth Missouri Cavalry, triumphed over the enemy in every conflict.

With regiments led by brave colonels, and brigades commanded with consummate skill and daring, the division in thirty days won a reputation unsurpassed in the service.

Though many of you have not received the reward to which your gallantry has entitled you, you have, nevertheless, received the commendation of your superior officers, and won the admiration and gratitude of your countrymen.

You will return to your homes with the proud consciousness of having defended the flag of your country in the hour of the greatest national peril, while, through your instrumentality, liberty and civilization will have advanced the greatest stride recorded in history.

The best wishes of your commanding general will ever attend you.

E. Upton,

Brevet Major-General commanding.

General Wilson, his own immediate commander, recognized Upton's services, and expressed in the following letter, written almost immediately after the close of the campaign, his opinion of his merits:

(Extract.)

Headquarters Cavalry Corps,

Military Department of the Mississippi, Macon, Ga., April 24, 1865.

Brigadier-General E. D. Townsend,

Assistant-Adjutant-General United States Army.

General:... I have the honor to recommend the following promotion:

Brevet Major-General Emory Upton, United States Volunteers, to be major-general, to date from April 1, 1865, for personal gallantry and good management in the engagement of Ebenezer Station, Alabama, also at Columbus, Georgia, where, by a night attack with three hundred men, he carried the rebel works, and captured the bridge over the Chattahoochee River, and took twelve hundred prisoners and fifty-two guns.

Throughout the entire campaign General Upton has exhibited the highest qualities of a general officer, and has demonstrated his fitness for advancement.

I am, general, very respectfully, your obedient servant,

James H. Wilson,

Brevet Major-General.

The duties which now fell to Upton's lot were those incident to that of all general officers of this period of approaching peace. The main business was economy. The burdens of the war were enormous, and the Government was no less anxious than the soldiers to get again into peaceful pursuits, and to reduce quickly the vast daily expenses of a war establishment. But, of course, this required time for its orderly evolution, and Upton's services were retained in the South till the middle of August. On the 1st of July he was ordered to report to General George Stoneman, commanding the Department of Tennessee, and was by him assigned to the command of the First Cavalry Division of that department, and on the 13th of July he was ordered to report to General A. C. Gillem, commanding the District of East Tennessee, for assignment to the command of all the cavalry of that district, with station at Lenoir, Tennessee. After a month's service he had completed the duty requiring his presence in this military department, and was relieved August 15th, and ordered by War Department General Order No. 130 to report to Major-General John Pope, commanding the Department of the Missouri. He had completed his active service in the field, which, characterized throughout by modest, patient, and persistent labor in preparation, and by every military virtue in actual conflict, had shed no less luster on our arms than honor and renown upon himself.

SERVICE IN COLORADO.—TACTICS.

The hardships and dangers of active campaigning were now happily ended, but the routine life of camp, varied only by a change of locality from time to time, was by no means as exciting as the life to which the troops had been accustomed. Their past years had been filled with the excitement of the march and the fever of battle, and they soon tired of the ennui of camp. The war being ended, there was now no sufficient reason in their minds why they should not at once return to their homes and attend to their families and their private interests.

It was a wise policy, therefore, on the part of the Government to muster them out of service as rapidly as possible. But, although this policy was almost essential, for the rapid decrease in the enormous expenditure which the army entailed, other considerations, connected with the unsettled condition of the Southern territory, demanded that a considerable force should yet be retained in the service until such new conditions of life should be evolved in the South as to insure a certain stability and become sufficiently adapted to the requirements of a brave but exhausted people.

These retained troops were, therefore, distributed throughout the Southern States in detachments of sufficient strength, and located at such points as were considered important for the purposes of the reconstructive measures undertaken by the Government. The new duties to which officers and men were assigned were far different from those to which they had been accustomed, and required of them patience and forbearance as well as the exercise of great discretion in the unsettled and sometimes turbulent region to which they were assigned. To the men at least this additional service was a great grievance, and an ever-present cause of unrest. Anxiety as to the condition of their families, and the deferred pleasures of a return to their homes, together with the difficulties attached to service in a community where the sentiment was hostile, all contributed to make them look forward with eagerness to their honorable discharge. To the officers there were compensating advantages in their continued employment, since the pay they received was ample to provide for their families, and they could readily obtain short leaves of absence to visit their homes and make provision for the coming day of discharge, or anticipate it under favorable opportunities by resigning.

General Upton's thoughts were still directed to the home of his youth. His parents, brothers, and sisters were still those to whom his affections most strongly turned. And so pure was the atmosphere of his home that its memories were the most potent of all influences which had so far kept him a noble man and a Christian soldier during the many vicissitudes of his active career.

Having completed the duty to which he was assigned, he was relieved from service in Tennessee on the 14th of August, and ordered to report to Major-General Pope, commanding the Department of Missouri, who assigned him to the command of the district of Colorado, with headquarters at Denver. Making but a short delay, he proceeded overland from Leavenworth to his new station, and we have in the following letter an account of the incidents of his journey:

Denver, October 1, 1865.

My dear Sister: I have the pleasure of announcing my arrival safe at my journey's end, after a long and somewhat weary march. We left Leavenworth on the 31st of August. Our outfit consisted of one four-mule wagon, a four-mule ambulance, two saddle-horses, and two mules. My only traveling-companion was Major Latta, my assistant adjutant-general. Having tents and a larder well supplied, we were in as good condition as any party that ever crossed the plains. After four days' march we arrived at Fort Riley, where we laid over one day, and were most handsomely entertained by General Sanborn. The escort of four hundred cavalry was nearly up here, and on the 6th of September, all preparations being made, we set out via the Smoky Hill for Denver.

On the third day we passed Fort Ellsworth, on the Santa Fé road, and entered the buffalo country. Of course, everyone has to "kill his buffalo"; and, mounted on a good horse, I made my first effort, which was a failure, as was also the second; but the third was a success.

You can scarcely imagine the excitement of a buffalo-chase. Mounted on a fleet horse, and armed with two or three revolvers, you single out a large herd and gallop toward it. They soon see you, and, taking the alarm from some old bull, follow him, generally running toward the wind. It is a beautiful sight to see them as they take the alarm and gallop away. With a large mane which gives them a terribly ferocious look, they seem to run as if on three legs, and you doubt not that a few seconds more will see you in their midst. But not so! After a sharp run you begin to approach them, your horse then takes the excitement, and, increasing his speed, closes upon them.

With the pistol cocked, and your eye upon a particular one, you close to fifteen or twenty feet and fire.

On they go, up steep hills and across deep ravines, the only effect of your shot being to increase their speed. The big bulls in the rear, apprehensive of their charge, hook up those which lag behind. With the dust in your face and your horse foaming, you close again and fire at the same buffalo, who, finally crippled or maddened by his wounds, lags behind, lunges at you as you approach, and, finally exhausted, stops to give battle. You have now won the day, and a good shot or two will close the struggle. Yet often as many as fifteen or twenty shots have to be fired before the vulnerable part is struck.

The heart is the only spot where one shot will kill. The skull seems to be as impenetrable as rock, and they will only shake the head when struck there. Their meat is very tough except the tenderloin, sirloin, and hump above the shoulders, which are quite delicate. These parts, in addition to the liver, heart, and tongue, are all that are used for meat, the remainder being left for the wolves.

The number of buffalo is astonishing, and often you find yourself among herds which extend for miles farther than the eye can reach.

The large gray wolf and the coyote always accompany them, and subsist mainly upon their flesh. Their howl has a most dismal sound, and awakens recollections of all the wolf-stories one has ever read. Prairie-dogs were frequent everywhere along our route. They live in villages—the different holes communicating with each other. They are about twice the size of a red squirrel, and I suppose from their chirp or bark take their name. The owl and rattlesnake come into their habitations without invitation.

Polecats were numerous on the plains, as were also antelope. Antelope-meat is the most delicate I ever tasted. The animal has short horns and a wonderful bump of curiosity, which often proves fatal to it; for many times it will approach close to you to ascertain definitely what you are. Once satisfied that there is harm, it will bound over the prairie at a marvelous speed. The hare or jack-rabbit is a queer little animal, which every few steps takes a high leap into the air, making his course very eccentric. We saw one tarantula, which belongs to the spider family. Its legs were two or three inches long and its body about four times the size of the largest black spider. Its bite is exceedingly venomous.

The plains are not so level as the Illinois prairies. Gulches and ravines, with deep beds of sand on their bottoms, frequently intersected our path. The Smoky Hill was nearly always to our left. Along its banks were a few cottonwood-trees, which were always a most welcome sight. The grass on the plains is very short but very nutritious. Water occurred about every twelve or fifteen miles, but sometimes we had to go twenty or more. At such times we experienced the same feelings of joy as travelers in the Sahara.

Geologically, the country was very interesting. The amount of denudation that has taken place was never more perceptible. We could frequently see ledges of rock on both sides of the river having the same elevation, while the river-bed was a hundred feet or more below. Evidently the immense amount of alluvium that it would require to fill this valley had been washed away, and doubtless for ages has been depositing in the Delta of the Mississippi. You have but to see the work Nature has done in wearing away the surface near one of the tributaries of the Mississippi, to readily believe the statement that two billion tons of detritus are annually deposited at the mouth of that great river.

Fremont's Fort or Buttes is a high table-land, two hundred feet above the surrounding country. Its surface is level, immediately underlying which is a stratum of rock about fourteen feet thick. Below this is a compact clay, I think (I did not have time to visit it). Time has worn the surrounding country away, but this table remains, to show where once was the original surface.

About the 27th of September we came in sight of Pike's Peak. It is a lofty monarch, with no associate to dispute its pre-eminence. Long's Peak came into view two days later, but, springing from the main chain, upon approach does not appear so high, although it is a few hundred feet higher.

On the 29th we got the first fine view of the mountains. I will not attempt to describe the beauty or sublimity of the scene, but will simply state that we stood on a high divide. Below was a beautiful table-land, extending to the base of the mountain; to our left was Pike's Peak, over thirteen thousand feet high; to our right was Long's Peak, with still greater altitude. Connecting them, a distance of nearly sixty miles, was a lofty range, its crest being nearly horizontal, but varied occasionally by bold and rugged summits, often a thousand feet or more above the range to the right of Long's Peak, and, extending as far as the eye could reach, appeared the lofty peaks of the Snowy Range. Three hundred feet below us lay the valley of Cherry Creek, which winds its way to the Platte, its course being visible by the trees that line its banks.

Add to this the fact that the sun had but just risen, and I will leave to your imagination to supply the picture. I never saw beauty and sublimity so magnificently blended, and felt that that one scene would more than compensate a year's toil and privation.

We arrived at Denver on the evening of the 29th. It lies at the mouth of Cherry Creek, and, though but six years old, has a population of four thousand. The people of the Territory are, of course, not so polished as Eastern people, but I have met many nice gentlemen. Prices are enormously high. Board at hotels is one hundred and thirty-five dollars per month, and other things in proportion. I shall soon go over my district on an inspection tour, and will have a fine opportunity to see the scenery, which I am satisfied rivals any in the world. I will write anything that may be of interest.

During his service in Colorado Upton made frequent inspections of his command, and, as was his custom, learned all that he could in regard to matters going on about him. The mining interests were, of course, all-absorbing to the people of Denver and its vicinity, and he neglected no opportunity of watching the development of the methods of mining and reducing the ore containing the precious metals. He foresaw that great changes would be brought about by the building of the Pacific Railroad, and that its completion would give a marked impetus to all branches of industry. To familiarize himself with the conduct of affairs in his military district and with the country, he visited Fort Halleck, from which he returned in October, and afterward made a trip to the mountain-region west of

137

Denver. He thoroughly examined the mineral region of Black Hawk, Central City, and Empire, and thus added greatly to his store of useful knowledge. On his return from his first expedition he sent the following letter to his superior military authority, wherein he exhibits the indignation of an honest man at the evidences of rascality that came under his notice:

Headquarters District of Colorado, Denver, Colorado, October 14, 1865.

My dear General: I beg leave to write you privately and unofficially in regard to my position as commanding officer of this district. In sending me out here you informed me that there were many abuses which you expected me to correct, and I was specially enjoined to retrench in every possible manner the expenses of the Government. As an officer I felt complimented by the trust you reposed in me, and I came out with the earnest desire to carry out, in the most minute particulars, your orders and wishes in regard to the expenditures of the Government. As an officer, I have always acted on the principle that there was but one course to pursue, and that was the straight line of duty. I was educated to believe that a public dollar was as sacred as a private one, and, to the extent that I am, or may be, its custodian, I will ever be faithful to my trust.

I find myself surrounded by a set of unscrupulous contractors and speculators, who regard the public money as their legitimate plunder. I will defeat their villainous schemes to the utmost, be the consequences to me what they may. I expect, in the fearless discharge of my official duties, to call down upon my head the venom of the entire class; and, as they have heretofore been all-powerful through the money they have stolen from the Government, I would not at any time be surprised were they to secure my removal. I therefore write you, general, to acquaint you with the situation. All that I ask is to be supported by my superior officers, and if, by the faithful discharge of my duties,

I secure their commendation, I shall care nothing for the abuse or vituperation of a horde of defeated speculators. I have just returned from an inspection of Fort Halleck and Camp Ward well, and will immediately forward official report.

I trust you will not consider that I have transcended the bounds of official propriety in addressing this communication.

During Upton's sojourn in Colorado, the reduction and reorganization of the army were engaging the attention of the Washington authorities. He knew that a very short service would soon terminate his career as a general officer of volunteers, and that he would then return to his lineal rank as a captain of artillery in the regular army.

He hoped, however, that in the reorganization he would be offered higher rank in one of the new regiments than his present lineal rank of captain, and he had assurances from distinguished officers, whose influence would have great weight, that his claims and services would not be overlooked. Nevertheless, being far distant from the seat of government, he well knew that there would be great pressure and strong influence brought to bear to advance the claims of other distinguished officers, and he therefore awaited the result with some anxiety. This anxiety would have been the less readily borne had not other matters pressed upon him and occupied every moment of his leisure time.

His profession was a continual study and employment for him. He loved it and devoted all his thoughts to it. While the war was in progress, he omitted no opportunity to study the details that are so often accepted unquestioned by ordinary men. Being eminently practical, and full of enthusiasm, he never hesitated to examine into the merits of the accepted practices of military movements and drill. Without being an iconoclast, he had no special reverence for established usages, simply because they had the authority of age. He preferred rather to test all things by the standard of utility, and in this spirit his mind was early directed to investigate the subject of the tactics for infantry troops. He came to the conclusion that the tactics in vogue were capable of great improvement, and, having frequent opportunities of testing the matter in the field, his opinions became strengthened and to himself conclusive.

In the spring of 1864 Upton began to formulate his ideas; and, having convinced himself that he had good grounds for the prosecution of his labors, he exhibited a practical illustration of his method for the evolutions of a regiment, by applying it to a battalion of the Second Connecticut Volunteer Artillery, in the presence of some distinguished general officers, a few days before the battle of Winchester. The success attending this trial, and the encouragement of those witnessing it, gave him the support he needed and heart enough to continue its development. Upon recovering from the wound he received at the battle of Winchester he sought service in the cavalry, in order to make himself familiar with this arm of the service; and the active campaign of Selma, in which the cavalry, armed with the Spencer carbine, acted mostly as mounted infantry, was of the greatest value to him in this important field of professional study. Tactics became the theme of his daily conversation, engrossed his mind almost to the exclusion of everything else, and he drew from every battlefield its important lesson.

We have before remarked that he possessed, in a remarkable degree, the *coup-d'oeil militaire*, by which the general features of the ground over which his troops were operating were impressed on his mind. This enabled him to foresee, in a measure, the possibilities of a battle, and to determine the probable movements of bodies of troops from one position to another. He imagined how this might best be done, taking into consideration the important element of time, and thus the probable and possible changes whereby the point of attack might be modified. This led him to consider the tactical movements by which these changes could be effected in the best manner and with the least confusion.

The authorized infantry tactics which were in use during the war were those of General Casey. They were based on the French tactics of 1831 and 1845, which had served also as the model of the tactics of General Scott and of Colonel Hardee, which preceded those of General Casey. This officer, in submitting his revision to the War Department, states: "Most undoubtedly there are still improvements to be made; but if the system here set forth shall in any manner cause our armies to act with more efficiency on the field of battle, and thus subserve the cause of our beloved country in this her hour of trial, my most heart-felt wishes will have been attained."

His system was used during the war. "Its merits and demerits had been subjected to the test of practice and experience," and Upton believed that there were sufficient reasons for a revision of the system. From the summer of 1864 until early in 1866 he studied this important subject in its theory and practice, and, having brought his labor to the point where he could present a new system to the military authorities for their approval or condemnation, he addressed the following letter to the Adjutant-General of the Army:

Headquarters District of Colorado, January 13, 1866.

Brigadier-General E. D. Townsend,

Assistant Adjutant-General United States Army.

Sir: I have the honor to request to be ordered to Washington, for the purpose of submitting to the Honorable Secretary of War, or to a Board of General Officers, to be convened by him, a new system of infantry tactics, with a view to its adoption for the infantry of the United States Army and the militia throughout the United States.

The system differs fundamentally from the old or French system, now in use, the unit being a front of four men. It is believed to be superior to the old system:

First. In abolishing the facings, and substituting wheeling by fours, hereby forming a column of fours, which you are enabled to form directly to the right, to the left, to the front, and, by wheeling about to the rear, into line, presenting always the front rank to the enemy.

Second. It takes no cognizance of inversions, and enables a battalion or brigade commander to form line in any direction with the utmost facility and ease.

Third. The number of commands has been reduced, and there is greater uniformity among them.

Fourth. It is more simple and less voluminous.

The system when presented will embrace the school of the soldier, the school of the company, instructions for skirmishers, the school of the battalion, evolutions of the brigade, and *corps d'armé*, and an appendix embracing evolutions of a battalion and brigade in single rank.

The feats of dismounted cavalry, armed with the Spencer carbine, in both the East and West, have demonstrated the fact that one rank of men so armed is nearly, if not quite, equal in offensive or defensive

141

power to two ranks armed with the Springfield musket. If this be admitted, a one-rank tactics becomes necessary for a certain proportion of troops, especially those designed to turn or operate on the enemy's flank.

The principle of fours enables troops to be brought on to the field in two ranks; to be expanded into a single rank by a simple command; and often to be maneuvered by the same commands as in two ranks.

This cannot be done by the old tactics without an entire change of commands.

I would state that three days before the battle of Winchester, in the presence of Brigadier-General D. A. Russell and other officers, I applied the principle of fours to a battalion of the Second Connecticut Heavy Artillery with complete success; and I have every confidence that were a Board of Officers to be convened at West Point, New York, I could, by a single application of the principle to the battalion of cadets, fully establish, to the satisfaction of the Board, the superiority above claimed.

I am, very respectfully, your obedient servant,

Emory Upton,

Brevet Major-General United States Volunteers.

While at Denver, attending to his duties as district commander, Upton had found time to perform all the necessary labor incident to this construction of his system, and, on February 11th, he writes to his sister:

"My tactics being finished, I have had quite a play-spell for the past week. I am now looking forward to the adoption of the tactics by the War Department, and, if successful, shall feel that I have established a solid reputation." But he soon found that his work was by no means completed, for on the 6th of April he again writes: "I have been extremely busy for the last six weeks, and it will no doubt surprise you when I tell you my tactics are not yet finished. The manuscript was completed sometime since, but the plates, which I supposed could be easily drawn, have occupied much more time than I anticipated. My knowledge of the rule and triangle has again been brought into requisition, and I feel quite like a student. It will require two or three weeks yet to complete the work, and have it in every sense ready for examination and publication. I shall then be ready to go East. Should

142

the work not be adopted, I shall have it published, but I have no misgiving, as the principle is new and entitled to consideration. Were my tactics but a revision of the present system, with a few unimportant movements added, I would not be sanguine, but as they aim at a complete revolution, and are far more simple, my confidence increases with every comparison I make. You need fear no evil effects upon me if disappointed, which I do not consider possible, as I have military men to deal with, who will adopt that system of tactics which is best for the army."

On the 30th of April, 1866, Upton was mustered out of the volunteer service, and returned to his rank in the regular army as captain of the Fifth Regiment of Artillery, to which he had been promoted February 22, 1865.

During the delay which he was authorized to take before joining his regiment, he visited his home, and was also permitted to come to Washington. While at the latter place he doubtless urged his views in regard to his tactics, and impressed them upon the authorities there with such effect as to secure the appointment of a Board for their consideration. Accordingly, on June 5, 1866, a Board, consisting of Colonels H. B. Clitz and H. M. Black, General Griffin, and Captain Van Horn, was convened to meet at West Point, New York, "for the purpose of recommending such changes in authorized infantry tactics as shall make them simple and complete, or the adoption of any new system that may be presented to it, if such change be deemed advisable. The Board will examine and report on any system of infantry tactics that may be presented to it; and the superintendent of the Military Academy will give it facilities for testing with the battalion of cadets the value of any system. Brevet-Colonel E. Upton, Fifth United States Artillery, is authorized to visit West Point, New York, to present his system to the Board."

General Griffin was, however, relieved from this Board June 8th, at his own request, and General R. B. Ayres, Captain Fifth Artillery, was detailed in his stead.

On July 18th General Upton was ordered to report to the President of the Board, and to hold himself in readiness to exhibit his tactics in the school of the battalion to the Board.

143

The result of the investigations of this Board, together with the indorsement of General Grant upon its report, is given in the following papers:

West Point, New York, January, 1867.

To the Adjutant-General U. S. A., Washington City, D. C.

General: The Board of Officers assembled at this place by virtue of Special Orders Nos. 264 and 272, of June 5th and 8th, 1866, War Department, Adjutant-General's Office, "for the purpose of recommending such changes in authorized infantry tactics as shall make them simple and complete, or the adoption of any new system that may be presented to it, if such change be deemed advisable," has the honor to report that, after a careful trial and scrutiny of the different systems presented, the Board has unanimously decided to recommend the adoption of Brevet Major-General Upton's system, a printed copy of which is herewith transmitted.

In making the examination, the Board suggested certain alterations, not affecting the general principles, which were readily concurred in by the author.

(Signed) H. B. Clitz,

Lieutenant-Colonel Sixth Infantry and Brevet Colonel, President of the Board.

R. B. Ayres,

Brevet Major-General United States Army. H. M. Black,

Major Seventh Infantry and Brevet Colonel. J. J. Van Horn,

Captain Eighth Infantry and Brevet Major, Recorder.

Headquarters Armies of the United States,

Washington, D. C., February 4, 1867.

Hon. E. M. Stanton, Secretary of War.

Sir: I have the honor to transmit herewith the report of the Board of Officers convened by Special Orders No. 264, War Department, Adjutant-General's Office, of date June 5, 1866, "for the purpose of recommending such changes in the authorized infantry tactics as shall make them simple and complete, or the adoption of any new system that may be presented to it, if such change be deemed advisable."

144

Having examined this report, I concur fully with the Board, and recommend the immediate adoption of *Upton's Infantry Tactics, Double and Single Rank*, as the text-book for the Military Academy and the standard tactics for the armies of the United States.

I have seen the system applied to company and battalion drills, and am fully satisfied of its superior merits and adaptability to our service; besides, it is no translation, but a purely American work. The Board by which it was examined and recommended was composed of officers of ability and experience, and I do not think any further examination by boards necessary.

Very respectfully, your obedient servant,

U. S. Grant, General.

Notwithstanding this gratifying recommendation of his system by the Board of June 5th, and its strong support by the General of the Army, opposition to it began to develop. This opposition naturally caused the War Department to hesitate before acting as the General of the Army had recommended, and to decide upon convening a new Board, composed of officers of such distinguished rank and ability that its recommendation would carry the greatest weight possible, and to which the views of officers opposed to the change were also to be submitted. Accordingly, the War Department issued the following order:

War Department, Adjutant-General's Office,

Washington, June 11, 1867.

Special Orders, No. 300.

A Board will assemble at West Point, New York, to take into consideration the system of infantry tactics prepared by Brevet Major-General E. Upton, United States Army, and will report its opinion, whether the said tactics should be adopted as the system for the armies of the United States, in lieu of all others. The Board will be composed as follows:

General U. S. Grant, United States Army; Major-General G. G. Meade, United States Army; Brevet Major-General E. R. S. Canby, United States Army; Brevet Major-General W. F. Barry, Colonel Second United States Artillery; Brevet Brigadier-General W. N. Grier,

Colonel Third United States Cavalry; Brevet Colonel H. M. Black, Major Seventh United States Infantry.

By order of the Secretary of War:

E. D. Townsend,

Assistant Adjutant-General.

This Board, after witnessing practical illustrations of Upton's tactics in the principles of the school of the company, by a company of cadets and by a company of engineer troops, and in those of the school of the battalion, and in skirmish-drill, during successive days, examined General Upton in such theoretical movements as were suggested by the members of the Board, and which could not be practically illustrated on the field. The Board then carefully considered the papers presented to it by Generals Casey, Morris, H. J. Hunt, and T. W. Sherman, and the reply of General Upton to the latter's objections to his system. This reply was as follows:

Washington, D. C., April 6, 1867.

Major George K. Leet,

Assistant Adjutant-General.

Sir: The communication of Brevet Major-General T. W. Sherman, Colonel Third United States Artillery, setting forth what he considers to be vital defects in my system of infantry tactics, having been referred to me by the General-in-Chief, I have the honor to submit the following remarks:

"The root of all the objections of importance that appears" is found in my omission or prohibition of manoeuvres by the rear rank.

The chief advantage claimed for the system is the adoption of a front of four men as a unit, the men of which, both front and rear rank, preserve or maintain in all movements a constant relation to each other.

The movement of "fours right or left about," whether in column or in line, places the troops facing in the opposite directions with the same freedom to manoeuvre as before, and with the front rank in front, which, as in all armies the best soldiers are to be found in the front rank, is not only decidedly advantageous, but abolishes all necessity for manoeuvres by the rear rank, especially when not in the presence of the enemy.

In the presence of the enemy, whether moving toward or from him, General Sherman maintains that the only "practicable mode" of facing, or marching in the opposite direction, is by the "individual about on the about face."

Two general cases can arise, viz., the troops may or may not be under the enemy's fire. If not under fire, then the "fours right or left about" is, of course, practicable, and retains all the advantages previously mentioned. If under fire, the tactics prescribe that the unity of the fours will be preserved as long as possible, and, as casualties occur in the front rank, the vacancies will be filled from the rear rank.

This provision then, theoretically, preserves the units until fifty per cent of the men are placed hors de combat, and it must necessarily follow that, no matter how severe the fire of the enemy may be, so long as the men are cool, remain in their ranks, and are under the command of their officers, just so long is the "fours right or left about" equally practicable with the "about face"; and further, in marching to the rear is preferable, inasmuch as all the men will be in their usual places, and the march of the line will be steady, whereas by the "about face" every man will not only be out of place, but will feel out of place; the poorest soldiers and marchers will be in front, and the march of the line will naturally be unsteady.

In support of this latter statement, it is but necessary to refer to any one's cadet experience, when he will remember that, in every instance when the battalion was faced about, maneuvered by the rear rank, not only were there crowding and unsteadiness, but that the precision of the movements never equaled that by the front rank.

General Sherman's assertion that the about face is alone practicable under the immediate fire of the enemy leads me naturally to infer that it is practicable at all times and under all circumstances. The principal object of tactics is to prepare or to dispose troops for battle. Now, in every battle, as every infantry officer of experience well knows, there is a time when all consideration for tactics is lost; it is when the opposing lines come within deadly range, and mutually engage each other with the determination to conquer. At this time everything depends upon the discipline and courage of the officers, and as success or defeat must ensue, whichever line is compelled to give ground will yield it in disorder and confusion, and not till it is rallied can tactics again be applied.

Under such circumstances, when the enemy is pouring in his fire at short range, not only is the "about face insuring the preservation of unity and solidity" impracticable, but it would be criminal for a colonel to command and attempt to execute "cease firing," "battalion about face," "forward march."

It is only under the circumstances here stated that the units of four can be destroyed, and, as in general regiments either recoil before sustaining a loss of fifty per cent, or else are victorious, I can see no weight to the objections raised. If the regiments recoil, the tactics will not be required till they are rallied in the rear; if they are victorious, they should be reformed immediately and again called off, which will give new and intact units. All the movements by fours are simple, quick, and mechanical. I have applied them to volunteer infantry and cavalry, and in the presence of the general-in-chief to the battalion of cadets, and never yet have seen any confusion or unsteadiness, even while teaching the principles.

General Sherman was at West Point last summer while the Tactical Board was in session. He presented to me then these same objections, and doubtless mentioned them to the Board. I know that the subject was thoroughly discussed, and that the Board decided that there was no necessity for manoeuvres by the rear rank.

The battalion of cadets was placed at the disposal of the Board, and whenever differences of opinion arose respecting an important principle the matter was settled by actual experiment. General Sherman states that there are other points which invite discussion, but, as he admits that they violate no important principle, he omits to remark them. To this it may be replied that no system of tactics could be elaborated, either by an individual or by a Board, to which some objections would not be found.

After a week's careful examination and deliberation, the Board, on the 15th of July, decided upon the following report:

The Board has fully considered the subject committed to it by the War Department's special order (No. 300), and, in addition to the study of the text, has witnessed the practical illustration of the most important principles involved in the new system of tactics. The only important omissions in its examination were the manual of arms in the

148

school of the soldier, the formation of squares in the school of the battalion, and all evolutions of the line.

The first varies, of course, with the arm, and for the same arm must, of course, be the same in all branches of the service; in the second (formation of squares), the principles are the same as in existing systems; and the third (the evolutions of the line) could not be practically illustrated by reason of the small number of troops present.

The general advantages of the new system are:

1. Its easy application to all the arms of the service, leaving nothing additional to any special branch, except the manual of the arm with which it fights, the adaptation of the words of command, the training of animals, and the management and care of the material with which it is equipped.

2. The readiness with which the principles may be acquired by new troops, abbreviating materially the time required to fit them for the field, and practically extending the effective term of service of the soldier. This is of great importance in its relation to the volunteer force, of which, in all great wars, our armies must be largely composed.

The special advantages are:

That it dispenses with the manoeuvres by the rear rank, by inversion, and the countermarch, and substitutes therefor rapid and simple conversion of front, and changes from column into line.

That it increases the number of modes of passing from the order in column to the order in line, facing in any direction; diminishes the time required for these changes, and preserves always the front rank in front; advantages of vital importance in the presence and under the fire of the enemy.

That it provides for all column movements required in an open country, and, by the column in fours, for the movements necessary in narrow roads, wooded or obstructed countries, without the extension incident to ordinary movements by the flank.

That it provides for a single-rank formation specially adapted to the use of breech-loaders.

That it provides for a system of skirmishing from double or single rank superior for offense or defense to any existing system.

The Board therefore recommends that the system of infantry tactics prepared by Brevet Major-General E. Upton, United States Army, be adopted as the system for the armies of the United States in the place of all others, and that, so soon as a sufficient time shall have elapsed for the correction of any errors of arrangement or detail, Boards for the special arms may be appointed for the purpose of adapting the tactics of their arms to the system now recommended.

U. S. Grant, General. George G. Meade,
Major-General, United States Army.
Edward R. S. Canby,
Brigadier and Brevet Major-General, United States Army
William F. Barry,
Colonel Second Artillery, Brevet Major-General,
United States Army.
William N. Grier,
Colonel Third United States Cavalry, Brevet Brigadier-General.
H. M. Black,
Major Seventh Infantry, Brevet Colonel, United States Army.
Approved, and referred to the Adjutant-General August 1, 1867.
E. M. Stanton, Secretary of War.

On the 1st of August, 1867, General Orders No. 73, from the Adjutant-General's office of the army, ultimately adopted the new system of infantry tactics for the United States Army, and for the observance of the militia of the United States, and on the 23d of August it was adopted and prescribed for the infantry forces of the State of New York.

During the period when the tactics were being examined and tested, and for a long time subsequently, Upton's system was the subject of a great deal of criticism, both favorable and unfavorable. Upton himself took no part in the public discussion, which was mainly carried on in the columns of the "Army and Navy Journal." He was, nevertheless, exceedingly interested in all that was said, and, naturally being open to conviction, he readily took the proper steps to correct whatever appeared to be defects in the minute details, but held unshaken ground upon the spirit of his system. He was overwhelmed with correspondence after the tactics were adopted, and received thousands of letters asking information upon hundreds of little unimportant points. All these letters were conscientiously answered, and his answers were always marked with his native courtesy. Often, when almost overcome by this sort of annoyance, he felt that, could he have foreseen the great labor and trouble which resulted, he would have hesitated long before undertaking such a task.

It will be seen, by a reference to the report of the Board of which General Grant was president, that this Board mentioned as among the advantages of Upton's system "its easy application to all arms of the service." The natural sequence of this commendation was an attempt made to assimilate the tactics of the three arms of the service, and to this end a Board was assembled at Fort Leavenworth, Kansas, about the 15th of September, 1869, "to practically test the systems heretofore adopted for the artillery, cavalry, and infantry arms of service; to reconcile all differences; to select the best forms of command, and of drum and bugle signals, and to submit for the approval of the War Department at as early a date as practicable the approved copies, in order that they may be printed in a uniform and convenient edition, and published for the government of the army and militia of the United States. The Board will be composed as follows: Major-General J. M. Schofield, United States Army; Brevet Brigadier - General J. H. Potter, Lieutenant-Colonel Fourth Infantry; Brevet Major-General Wesley Merritt, Lieutenant-Colonel Ninth Cavalry; Major James Van Voast, Eighteenth Infantry; Brevet Colonel John Hamilton, Major First Artillery."

General Upton undertook the revision of his tactics, and in his endeavor to overcome the difficulties imposed upon him by the requirements of this assimilation, although very much hampered, he nevertheless succeeded in removing all of the more serious obstacles.

The labors of this Board did not completely solve the problem, nor finally remove all the difficulties. Its proceedings were ultimately submitted to another board, composed of General Upton, Colonels DuPont and Tourtellotte, and Captain Bates, which was convened at West Point early in 1873.

Colonel DuPont had been a member of a board of officers convened to reconstruct the artillery tactics, and there is no doubt that General Upton had the highest opinion of his ability, which, joined with his eminent services during the war as an artillery officer, greatly influenced his selection. He was one of those careful and exact men whose decision is based only on a searching and comprehensive examination. He was well versed in the meaning of words, and, before consenting to their employment, he weighed well the definition of terms. While his untiring criticisms somewhat prolonged the work, the value of his services, in insuring greater accuracy, in diminishing the number of assailable points of adverse criticism, and in his practical and theoretical knowledge, is beyond all question. The artillery tactics, as they stand today, are indebted to him for many marked improvements. Colonel Tourtellotte, aide to General Sherman, was a lawyer by profession, and had been a gallant officer of volunteers during the war, rising to the rank of brigadier-general by brevet. He possessed most excellent judgment, and a temperament that fitted him to decide dispassionately upon disputed points. Captain Bates, instructor of cavalry tactics at the Military Academy, was thoroughly acquainted with the tactics of this arm, and could test proposed innovations before consenting to their adoption. General Upton was full of the spirit of his subject. He had had experience in the tactics of the three arms during active service, and was now engaged in giving to the cadets theoretical instruction in all. Impetuous by nature, he was obliged, by the character and ability of his associates, to prove every point, and to establish by sound reason the rationale of each new proposition. Previous to and during the existence of this Board, he corresponded freely with his friend and associate Colonel DuPont, and his letters exhibit the animus that controlled him. A few extracts, to exhibit the progress of his work, the changes in his views, and his satisfaction in his completed labor, are here introduced:

West Point, June 30, 1870.—I fear that the assimilation of tactics will be detrimental.

March 17, 1871.—While there is no objection to assimilation, it should only take place when it will not prejudice either arm; but to inflict a single movement in infantry or artillery simply because it is necessary in cavalry is absurd.

April 17, 1871.—No better Board to revise the artillery tactics could be appointed than the one you mention, leaving me out. Could Seymour, Morgan, and yourself be detailed, the Board to convene here, where we have light, mortar, siege, and sea-coast batteries, you could get up a tactics which would bear the test of years. I am really too busy to have the additional labor of a Board imposed upon me, but I could assist your Board very materially in assimilating the artillery to the infantry, where it can be done without prejudice to the artillery. Besides, I would read your work over as you progress, and, if I discovered any inconsistencies, I would point them out. Teaching the tactics of the three arms enables me to discover many absurdities which could be done away with.

January 1, 1872.—The Academy is now on a splendid footing. Ruger is a model soldier, and possesses every qualification to make a good super-intendent, and he is thoroughly liked. The young blood has a clear majority on the Academic Board, and, while there are no cliques or cabals, the action is generally satisfactory. I can tell you with all confidence that, in future, cadets must have some sense to graduate.

December 29, 1872.—The infantry tactics are to stand according to my revision, and the artillery and cavalry tactics are to be assimilated as far as possible. We can devote from six to nine hours daily, and finish the work, I hope, inside of three weeks. Your work will terminate with the artillery tactics, which we will take up about January 15th.

March 1, 1873.—The work done with Bates in cavalry tactics comprises school of platoon mounted, troop dismounted and mounted, half of troop skirmish-drill mounted. By the 15th will finish battalion, and a week later brigade and division, which will embrace all to the appendix. The cavalry tactics will be a success, their mobility being quite equal to the infantry.

March 13, 1873.—Cavalry tactics progressing finely, and Tourtellotte begins to see that assimilation is not hopeless, after all.

March 14, 1873.—Tourtellotte delighted with the assimilation, and will be more pleased still when he sees the troop and skirmishers. All the movements by fours we have proved by experiment in the riding-hall, and, what is more gratifying, we have fully satisfied ourselves that in wheeling about by fours in line there is ample space for chiefs of platoon and file-closers to pass between the fours pending the movement. This is a great triumph, and completes, in every respect, the assimilation to infantry.

153

The correspondence up to the next quoted extract referred mainly to DuPont's labors in artillery tactics, expressing gratification at his progress, and showing that all the credit for these tactics belonged to DuPont himself. The labors of the Board practically ceased in July, only minor matters requiring attention, and these received at Upton's hands the most careful study.

August 12, 1873.—With regard to Tourtellotte's fear that General Sherman will become impatient "at the delay in completing the minor points," I am resolved not to be stampeded. It is our reputation that is at stake, and the only safe course is to make haste slowly by being satisfied at each step that we are right. The fact is, that our work all around has had so many tests that we cannot make any gross mistakes.

September 1, 1873.—Battalion drills begin today, and afford another opportunity to verify our work.

October 31, 1874.—Tactics are printed, and copies sent to you. [Colonel DuPont was at that time in Europe.] We have at least given our successors a basis upon which to work.

November 23, 1874.—The statuettes sent me by you are beautiful; a most becoming ornament to a soldier's quarters, and as an evidence of your esteem they will be appreciated all my life. They will remind me of much hard work, and of a devotion to duty on your part, which I wish the Government might suitably recognize. I fear, however, we shall have to find our recompense in the satisfaction which results from contemplating one's labors. That may not be inconsiderable, for I firmly believe that the three books will stand many years as an evidence of our labor, and, in your case, of the midnight oil often consumed in their production. The artillery tactics have been sent to Washington, but have not been out sufficiently long to elicit criticism. I sent General Barry a copy. He spoke favorably of them, but regretted that we did not give the Board of which he, Hunt, and French were members any credit. They, however, in my judgment, are no more entitled to it than Anderson and the French writers whose works he translated. Certainly there is not a single paragraph in your artillery-work identical with one in any previous book.

February 25, 1875.—I received, a few days since, a copy of General Sherman's letter to General [Henry Jackson] Hunt in reply to the latter's criticism on artillery tactics, and, as it may interest you, I send you a copy.

154

Hunt, I am told, began with the color of the cover of the book, and then went through it in a savage spirit, leaving us nothing to stand upon. General Sherman's reply has answered him completely. There has been little or no criticism in the *Journal*, beyond what I have sent you. General Barry has written me several letters, taking it apparently very hard that we in our preface did not give the French, Barry, and Hunt Board all the credit of producing the new work. I told him that we concluded that we could not give one party credit without mentioning a vast number equally entitled to it. He finally admitted that they could only claim originality in the school of the battery dismounted; that the detachment as a unit was original, and that in consequence of the simplicity of this device the volunteer artillery was made efficient in one tenth of the time required by former tactics. He also repeated Hunt's insinuations that I derived my principle of "fours" from the artillery, and, as might be inferred, all the benefits resulting from the recent improvements in tactics could be referred back to the invention of the detachment. I told him that before their Board assembled the batteries must have had a system of manoeuvres on foot, and, to enlighten me, he replied that some used infantry drill, while all the horse-batteries used the dismounted drill of the cavalry— in other words, they wheeled and maneuvered by "fours."

As the detachment had but a front of four men, I replied that their unit differed from the "four" only in name, and that the source of their inspiration must have been the cavalry. He also felt aggrieved because we appropriated the Gatling drill. To this I replied that, as you were a member of the Board which got it up, you felt at perfect liberty to use it, and, further, that either of us could have prepared it in three or four days. I believe he is satisfied that we were right in doing as we did.

The labors of the Board being completed, and the manuscript of the three tactics having been approved and sent to the printer, the subject of tactics was settled for the army for the time being by the publication of General Order No. 6, Headquarters of the Army:

War Department, Washington, D. C., July 17, 1873.

The revision of Upton's infantry tactics by the author, and the tactics for artillery and cavalry (including the proceedings of the Board—Major-General Schofield, President—instituted by General Orders No. 60, Headquarters of the Army, Adjutant-General's Office, Series of 1869) assimilated to the tactics for infantry, pursuant to instructions from the General of the Army, by Lieutenant-Colonel Emory Upton,

First Artillery, Instructor of Tactics, United States Military Academy; Captain Henry A. DuPont, Fifth Artillery, commanding Battery F, Fifth Artillery; Captain John E. Tourtellotte, Seventh Cavalry, Colonel and Aide-de-Camp to the General; Captain Alfred E. Bates, Second Cavalry, Assistant Instructor of Cavalry Tactics, United States Military Academy; having been approved by the President, are adopted for the instruction of the army and militia of the United States.

To insure uniformity, all exercises, evolutions and ceremonies not embraced in these tactics are prohibited, and those therein prescribed will be strictly enforced.

William W. Belknap,

Secretary of War.

It would be foreign to the purpose of this memoir to consider the objections which have been made against the assimilation of the tactics. Professional men may reasonably differ in regard to the details of their profession, and these differences may sometimes become the more pronounced in proportion as the particular point at issue is the more insignificant. In course of time, as the arms change and become more efficient, modifications of tactics will necessarily arise. Leaving aside, therefore, all questions relating to origin, authorship, and importance of the changes that have taken place in the tactics of the three arms of the service since the war, we may briefly sum up the influence that General Upton unquestionably exerted in this respect.

Early in his career as a regimental commander, and while in active service, he became convinced that certain improvements could be devised for the more rapid formation of troops from line into column and from column into line. He believed in the value of the unit of four men as comrades in battle, and made it the basis of his new system. He discarded what was known as "inversions" by having no fixed right or left, these directions being the actual right or left of the given formation. He simplified his commands and greatly abbreviated the subject-matter of his text. Thoroughly convinced by theoretical considerations and actual observation, he exhibited his system to some of his brother officers by actual manoeuvres of a regiment of volunteers in the field. He sought service in the cavalry and pursued his observations during a most active campaign, considering every movement in all its aspects, and discussing its bearing with whomsoever would listen to him during the night in camp. Deeply impressed with the importance of his labor and its value to our troops, he digested the whole, and promulgated it into a system of infantry tactics. It received the unequivocal indorsement of two boards, composed of the best and most capable officers, and was finally adopted by the President as the American system of tactics.

The following extracts from a letter sent him by an officer whose professional knowledge and ability are unquestioned are worth preserving in this connection:

St. Louis, July 20, 1870.

... I can state my individual opinion, as concerns the question of the credit due you on the *Tactics*. I do not consider the "formations," or (better, may be) the "orders," in which men may be placed, as the peculiar property of any individual. The order in column, in line, and in their subordinate formations, are the common property of the world. If a man starts an elementary system, it is his obligation to show how to bring about these orders or formations. This is the cart-horse part of the business of authorship. Now, I know nothing of the laws in the question of copyright.

But I say that, so far as I am actually informed, you are entitled to the full credit of the following proposition: "Upton was the first to assert and apply that fours in double rank was the smallest unit that could be wheeled into column, and thus get rid of the lock-step in the flank marches that a line of men might have to take up."

This may appear a small declaration, but you will remember that it is more than can be said of Scott, of Hardee, of Casey, or of any other tactician before you. Hardee could form fours (in facing). This he got from the French. Cooke could wheel fours (single-rank cavalry), and may be suggested that double-rank infantry could do the same thing, but how to obtain the "distance" I have yet to see that he found out. Hunt always had fours practically in his artillery detachments of cannoneers, but it was a simple necessity of their having a commandant. He took no advantage of it to obliterate the lock-step.

You have combined all the advantages, and you must be remunerated.

Upton was not called upon to consider the subject of tactics again until the matter forced itself upon the attention of military men, by more recent improvements in the weapons devised for infantry, and, as this matter has an important bearing upon his professional reputation and his estimate as a tactician, we will return to the subject in another chapter.

THE END

Discover more lost history from BIG BYTE BOOKS